EARLY PRAISE FOR

THE NEWBORN BABY BLUEPRINT

"This gem of a book is like finding a wise, authentic, funny friend who's also a pediatrician. It's the perfect gift for yourself or for anyone you love who is expecting a baby or navigating the early years of parenting."
—Pam E.

"Finally a handbook that addresses what every new parent needs to know before and after baby arrives! A quick, informational read that you'll refer to time and time again."
—Gwen P.

"This is a wonderful resource for new parents! Enough of the predictable and preachy books out there on parenting. *The Newborn Baby Blueprint* is a book for all of us with real lives—facing the amazing highs and lows of early childhood parenting. Well done!"
—Kris M.

The Newborn Baby Blueprint

The Newborn Baby Blueprint

Preparing to Care for Your Infant and Yourself

WHITNEY CASARES, M.D., M.P.H., F.A.A.P.

Modern Mommy Doc

THE NEWBORN BABY BLUEPRINT

First edition: April 2018

ISBN 978-1717086020

This publication contains the opinions and ideas of its author. It is intended to provide helpful and informative material. It is sold with the understanding that the author and publisher are not engaged in rendering medical, health or any other kind of personal professional services in the book. The reader should consult his or her medical, health, or other competent professional before adopting any of the suggestions in this book or drawing inferences from it.

The author and publisher specifically disclaim all responsibility for any liability, loss, or risk, personal or otherwise, which is incurred as a consequence, directly or indirectly, of the use and application of any contents of this book.

Cover design by Pinegate Road

For information about special discounts for bulk purchases or to book a live speaking event with the author, please contact Modern Mommy Doc at 1-503-928-8188 or info@modernmommydoc.com.

DEDICATION

To my exhausting, amazing children, who have educated me in the
ways of motherhood far more than any official training ever could. I
wouldn't want my life any other way.
To my husband, who balances my enthusiasm and persistence with a
steady dose of humor and reality.
And to my parents, who have always dreamed alongside me and for
me, teaching me to value hard work and vision equally.

CONTENTS

ACKNOWLEDGMENTS

This book would not have been possible without the support and input of so many people. Special thanks to Mari Kay Evans-Smith, M.D. and Bruce Birk, M.D., my pediatrician colleagues who provided early content help; to Ellen Portait, R.N., and Jennifer Siebold, N.P., who provided feedback on lactation topics; to Reagan Cannon and Christie Artis, who helped with early website conceptualization; to Evernew Photography, who brought the Modern Mommy Doc vision to life visually; to Chelsea Smith, who helped with photography and website videography; to Aric Armon, who worked with me on logo design; to Caroline Ghiossi, who gave me the current pregnant mom perspective; to Kelsey Chronkhite at Pinegate Road, my talented website and book cover designer; to Melanie Casares, who helped me immensely with initial editing; to Holly Montcith, my copy editor; to Valerie Valentine, my proofreader; and to my husband, who has always been my best editor-in-chief.

1

INTRODUCTION

*The moment a child is born, the mother is also born. She never
existed before. The woman existed, but the mother, never. A
mother is something absolutely new.*
—Rajneesh

Yesterday, I heard my almost-eighteen-month-old toddler wake up,
and I hurried upstairs to get her. She looked up, smiled a huge, toothy
grin, and babbled some funny phrase about bananas and her bunny as
she realized it was time to start the day. As I held her for the first time
that morning, rubbing her back and gazing at her little fingers resting
on her cheek, I thought, "How did I get so lucky?"

That would not have been my sentiment as a new parent, now four
and a half years ago, when my first child was born. Even though I knew
what to expect medically with a new baby, I felt blindsided at first by
the fatigue, stress, and emotions that come with being a new mom.

My first daughter was what we lovingly referred to as a "hater": she
hated the swing, the pacifier, the carrier, the baby wrap, the bassinet,
the car seat, the bouncy chair, and the activity mat. I know, because we
tried them all. We eventually nicknamed her "Limoncello," in refer-
ence to the lemony Italian liquor, for her ability to be super sweet when
peaceful yet strong and sour at many other times.

I started to wonder after a few weeks what was making her that
way. Was I too anxious? Did I not have her on an adequate sleep
schedule? Was there something I was eating, wearing, doing, or not
doing? Would it ever end, and would I ever get sleep again? I am a
pediatrician, and yet I searched the internet just like every other parent
of a "hands-on" baby for a way to fix her.

Back in the throes of colic and tears (or even before they came), I

1

wished that someone had sat me down and gone through what to expect in the first weeks and months in a very real, unfiltered way. *The Newborn Baby Blueprint* is my best attempt at doing just that for you.

My greatest joy in my pediatrics practice is working with new and expectant moms, helping them build confidence with their little ones and finding the resources they need. I see many consistent themes as women transition into motherhood, the most common of which is shock at the paradigm shift when they find themselves suddenly responsible not only for the well-being but also the survival of another human being—shock at the lack of information they had going into the whole baby thing.

Sure, moms-to-be learn a lot of tips and tricks about baby gear and birth plans, but because sometimes it's hard to think past what's right in front of them, they never get past the whole labor-and-delivery-planning mind-set. After baby arrives, they feel, well, blindsided. And alone. And a little frustrated that people definitely told them at some point that "being a mom will be hard" but never said specifically what was so hard about it and what they could do to make it better.

I started thinking about how to help other moms like me enter motherhood with the practical, realistic information they need—the information I needed—about how to prepare themselves, their partners, and their families for the major change they are about to face.

In *The Newborn Baby Blueprint*, I think you'll find the answers to the deeper questions you have about becoming a mom—the haunting questions that all of us have. You know, the ones about how you are actually going to *do this*. And I think you'll find a lot of reality and reassurance.

The first two weeks, two months, even six to seven months can be tough with a little one. There is so much transition. The learning curve is incredibly steep. It's intimidating. In the end, though, there is joy—completely magical, over-the-top, amazing joy.

SECTION I

DOING YOUR RESEARCH

2

GETTING YOUR MIND RIGHT

All I want is a cup of coffee: hot, dark coffee to start the day. But the baby is crying, the toddler is whining, and, even though I'm doing my best, still I can't seem to make anyone happy in this moment.

This morning, I went to change the little one's diaper, and the poop came spewing out at me, faster than I could react. It shot into my hair; it peppered the sheets of my bed; it somehow ended up on all the clean diapers I had placed next to her. It was everywhere. Like a bomb of mustard popcorn had exploded. It was disgusting. At least it smelled like popcorn, but it was still disgusting.

Now we're in the kitchen, and I must have turned the stove up too high because those eggs cooked way too fast and they are looking a little charred. "Yuck. Those eggs are *not* fresh," says my big girl. "I would like peanut butter and jelly, not *that*!" Tears, a whole four-year-old body flailing to the ground out of protest. The plate almost crashes before I can lunge for it.

That's being a mommy. Not always, but a lot of the time. Which can be hard to come to grips with before it becomes your reality.

If you are like me, you've had a job, you've traveled, you have somewhat (or a lot) of a social life. When your kids come, that tends to change a little bit, but it's not forever. You don't have to lose yourself when you become a parent. You do, though, have to adjust your expectations. You will have fun again, you will have date nights, you will at some point (kind of) get back to who you were before you became Mommy or Daddy.

Right now, though, it's time to dig in your heels and expect many tough days and nights. You're in store for moments of complete bliss, to be sure, but being a parent can be, well, annoying at times. You don't have your freedom, you lose control of your schedule, you get lost in a sea of feeding and pooping and sleeping—then you do it all again. Is it worth it? Absolutely. Is it hard? You betcha.

Better to be mentally prepared for a period of awkward transition than to expect smooth sailing from the get-go. Becoming a parent, just like starting any new and challenging job, usually involves a steep learning curve. Here are my top tips for getting your mind right before baby comes.

ACCEPT CHAOS

Embrace the fact that your home will not be a serene haven of adult life for several years. If you have toys and play mats and kids' stuff all around, do not stress out that your house will never be as neat and tidy as it once was. It won't be. That's life. Congratulations, you have a child now. Where there was serenity, there will now be a little being full of joy and life (and noise and mess).

Instead of aiming for peace and quiet, figure out how to get ahold of yourself when you're stressed out by your chaotic little one or your chaotic environment. Kind of amazingly, your neurons are completely connected to your newborn's when he or she is first born, so it pays in a multitude of ways to find calm. No pressure, right? But seriously, your level of stress or nonstress impacts your baby's disposition.

What can you do about it when the eggs are burning and the diapers are overflowing?

Imagine yourself sitting on top of a huge glass bubble. Inside it, you and your child are having your moment. You can see what's going on, but you're not a part of it; instead, you're an observer. You notice what's going on before your eyes, but it's going on in front of you, not to you, like you're watching yourself in a movie. Suddenly, as you breathe and observe, you're not so caught up in how horrible everything is right then. You have emotional distance and gain some objectivity.

Yogis and psychologists call this meditating; I call it "Out of the Bubble." It's just a concrete metaphor for removing yourself emotionally from the situation—even just for a moment—so you can get a little perspective.

Of course, breathing in and out and using imagery are not going to solve every problem you will ever have as a parent, and you may not even be able to use this strategy every time you have a crazy day. When you can use it, though, you'll feel yourself relax and develop mindfulness. You'll build resilience in yourself and your kids as they watch you learn how to cope in stressful situations.

Using breathing and mindfulness is an amazing trick for reducing stress in new parents specifically, because those early "dog days" of parenting seem sometimes to be never-ending.

You'll hear the clichés from those who have already lived it: "It'll be over before you know it. That time is so precious; don't wish it away." Of course, they'll be right. But until you make it over that steep, dry mountain of early parenting, over to the lush, green (in some ways easier) valley that's waiting for you, it won't feel brief, or precious, or wistful. It will feel, literally, like poop and eggs and spit-up all over your hair. Learn to laugh and breathe. It's all you can do.

THERE ARE ALWAYS SECOND CHANCES

The most confident parents learn quickly to give themselves a break if they don't do things "just right." Everyone has moments when she worries more than she wants to or doesn't parent like a pro (or even like her more experienced parent friends do).

There will be times you will plan an outing only to realize you should have stayed in. One day, you will scrounge around in your diaper bag while out to lunch with a wailing, pee-soaked baby and realize you have no more diapers. A day will come when you realize you totally missed the boat on why your baby was so fussy. Accept your mistake and move on. We all do that stuff. Seasoned parents *continue* to do that stuff.

Even doctors miss the obvious sometimes. One of my pediatrician partners didn't realize his daughter's wrist was broken for a week, until she finally told him, "I need an X-ray." I missed my daughter's case of pinworms (yes, you read that right) for a whole month. If you feel confused or regretful early on, you're in good company. Just remember that when you mess up, you learn something, and you'll be better at it tomorrow.

ONE DAY YOU'LL THINK YOU HAVE IT ALL
FIGURED OUT . . .

There will be a day when you think you have it figured out. Then everything will change again, and you'll need to go back to the drawing board.

As your child develops, the tricks that worked to help her sleep, to entertain her and to help her grow will evolve as she does. One day, she'll love the swaddle; one day later, it's the sleep sack. The change in preference is not the big deal—it's the two weeks it takes to figure out the issue keeping her (and you) awake all night. The good news is that, as you get to know your little nugget, those transitions will be easier and easier.

The most successful new parents I meet try not to (1) expect things always to stay the same, (2) get irritated by every developmental stage a child goes through, or (3) expect the transition through those stages to progress in a straight line, instead of a messy zigzag.

The second no-no is a trap reserved mostly for first-time moms and dads, but second-timers fall into it from time to time, too, especially when they have more than one kid to juggle. I see it a lot in my practice. Although many new parents understand pretty quickly that feeding troubles and sleepless nights are just part of the game, some bang their heads against the wall with what seems like shock and terror as each new developmental stage (and headache) arises.

They can't seem to accept that certain childhood behaviors are just a normal part of growing up. And although I'm impressed by their tenacious desire and willingness to problem-solve, sometimes I think they've been misled along the way by their friends and by society.

No one has bestowed upon them this parenting pearl: yes, we can prevent and address a lot of health issues that come up for newborns and young kids, but some things (like cluster feeding, sleep regressions, and colic) are more about muddling through with the right perspective than they are about finding quick-fix solutions. Some things just take time to get better. (Major caveat here: if you have a serious health concern about your child and/or are worried about her safety or about potential illness, contact your doctor right away.)

Mommy Guilt is one of the worst parenting tricks in the book. There you are, perfect little baby in hand, and *wham!*—in will come Mommy Guilt, making you feel like a failure when you're not producing enough milk, taunting you when you leave your baby for the first time, gnawing at you, making you feel like you must not be doing enough to stimulate, soothe, protect, what-have-you your little one.

It can be worse when they start to get a little older. When my youngest daughter turned one year old, she perfected the "Mommy don't go" cry, which usually consisted of "Mom, Mom, Mom, Mom, Mom, Mom" over and over again while she clung to my pant leg. It reliably happened when I was heading out to my job in the morning or when I was all geared up to work out. It hardly ever happened to my husband (I'm sure it did, I just didn't notice it, because I only have room in my brain for my guilt, not his as well). It was enough to make me cry in my car occasionally.

What are our choices as modern mothers when Mommy Guilt comes barging in?

The Martyr Route

We could never take time for ourselves. Never take the time to hang out with friends. Never take an adult vacation. Never feel like we're inconveniencing our partners or other caregivers.

It's an option I see a lot of parents take. I could, too. But I know where that path leads us, and it's dark and lonely and kinda muddy.

Plus, the Mommy Guilt itself doesn't serve us well. We're less physically and mentally healthy. We're faster to get irritated and lose our cool with the kids. We're—let's face it—a pretty sad example of the balance we hope our girls or boys will have in their own lives.

The Balanced Route

We can figure out what the real issue is, what scares us so much when we prioritize ourselves as much as the other people and obligations we have.

As you think about your new baby coming into the world, consider this one of the major parenting philosophy choices you make. Just like you'll set an example for your children to be kind and to be hardworking, you'll also set an example when it comes to balance and perspective.

Now, somewhere along the way, someone (read: usually a partner or an older family member) is going to make you question your decision to make self-care a priority.

We live in a society where perfect motherhood is mystified and celebrated and expected to happen on its own. Our social media posts are just a little too glossy and polished. Our celebrities make motherhood seem like a goddess dream. Magazines sell us on the fake assumption that if we get all the right gear and plan it all out, we'll get an A+ in parenting class. Set that in contrast with the messy reality of our day-to-day lives—we're bound to be uneasy and a bit ashamed.

Overwhelmed by the Motherhood Goddess Myth herself, New York City mom Margaret Nichols said it well when she spoke about the pressure to do things "just right" in *Time* magazine's cover story on the issue: "What I've learned is there are some things you can control, but there is a lot you can't. We just have to give ourselves a break and do the best we can."

Where is the evidence that working or taking some time for self-care (I'm not talking about going out every single night 'til dawn; I'm talking about taking consistent time for ourselves to regroup and reboot) actually damages our kids? Wait for it . . . *it's not there.*

Three things that actually do matter?

Providing Consistency

Tons of families come to my clinic asking about family dinners. They've heard a lot about their importance on social media and in books they've read, but the truth is, family dinners are just one example of providing times throughout the day and week that our kids can count on. Kids thrive on routine. There are always times we have to make adjustments, but if you build in planned times to connect that your kids can count on, that is more important than you being physically present with your children twenty-four hours a day.

Being Focused

It's so much worse to spend all day on your smartphone while your child tries to get your attention than it is to take care of what you need to do in a chunk of concentrated time and then give your kids the undivided attention they deserve. Make the time you spend with your children purposeful instead of distracted, and you'll enjoy it more and not wish you were somewhere else the whole time. If you've taken your own time to take care of yourself, this won't be such a challenge.

Sharing the Load

Allow other caretakers in your child's life to be equal players who provide the same level of consistency you do. I promise, they will rise to the occasion and have a stronger relationship with your baby as a result.

Nine out of ten weekends in our house, my husband makes waffles and takes the kids to the park while I do something solo. The next morning, we switch, and I do something special with them. Each gets time to reboot, and we're less resentful of the other's free time, plus we get some individual moments with our kids to make memories.

Mommy (and Daddy) Guilt will be hard to avoid, but the reality is that it just doesn't do us any good. Take care of yourself so that you can take care of the other people in your life with an equal measure of love and commitment.

3

GEARING UP YOUR GEAR

My husband won't let me live it down. We were out on our first lunch date postbaby with the little one in tow. We had just come from the doctor's, two days into doing this on our own without the doting of hospital nurses, and though we were a little intimidated, we followed the advice of our pediatrician and braved a not-so-crowded restaurant in the middle of the day for burgers and fries.

We were there for less than an hour, and my daughter slept the entire time, but onlookers must have thought we were planning to stay the weekend: we brought along a mini breastfeeding pillow, six diapers, two packs of wipes, a nursing cover, hand sanitizer, an extra swaddle blanket (or three), a small white noise machine, the stroller, and, of course, the car seat.

It was, looking back, hilarious. All my stuff barely fit on the bench beside my baby. We didn't use any of the items we carted in from the back of the car (other than the car seat, where our infant lay quietly snoozing, oblivious to our neurosis about being overly prepared).

I have a picture of myself from that day, sheepishly smiling into the camera. A few short weeks before, I had been in nesting mode, reading review after review about the perfect this and that and the other baby item. When my mom came to my house and saw that we registered for a wipe warmer, she burst out laughing.

"You're kidding me, right? No baby needs that."

But I was convinced, just like most other parents-to-be who get sucked into the billion-dollar baby business brouhaha, that I needed it all. When I took all that unused junk to Goodwill a few years later (when I was preparing for my second child to arrive), I finally believed her good advice: you are going to get and buy a ton of stuff when your new baby is born. You won't need most of it. If you do end up needing it, it's usually only a click away.

Here's my list of the top ten things I recommend actually investing in ahead of time.

One Small Box of Newborn Diapers

You don't know how big your son or daughter will be, and you'll be sad if you have a storage shed full of newborn diapers when your child is a size 1 within a week of birth. You can *always* get more really quickly.

Tons of Wipes

My favorite brand is Pampers Sensitive. I also like Water Wipes, especially during a diaper rash.

Vitamin D Drops

Breastfed babies need 400 International Units of vitamin D per day until they reach one year of age. Carlson's D Drops or Baby D Drops are great options.

Swaddle Blankets

I love the look of silky swaddle blankets, and these can serve a number of purposes (think car seat cover or diaper change pad in a pinch, burp cloth, breastfeeding cover). For actually swaddling a baby, blankets that are a little less slippery tend to be a better choice.

Zip-Up Sleepers

No snaps, no buttons. When your baby is a newborn, you want easy access to all those poopy diapers, especially at 2 a.m. I will never forget my husband fumbling with my daughter's tiny snaps in the middle of the night, mumbling under his breath about the makers of such "ridiculous getups." He was right. Lose the fancy clothes while at home until about three months. Stick with zip-up sleepers at night.

A Place for Your Baby to Sleep

Many parents use a bassinet next to their bed or an American Academy of Pediatrics-approved co-sleeper for the first few weeks of their baby's life for easy feeding during the night. It's fun to buy a fancy crib and decorate a fancy nursery, but your baby doesn't care as much as you do about it. You want convenience as a new mom, not aesthetics.

A Car Seat

There are *tons* of options out there. After a few months, you'll probably end up taking your baby out of the car seat to carry him or her around, so, my best advice is, don't overthink it. Lots of companies work hard to sell you on features like longevity or lightness, but babies outgrow car seats very quickly. They usually don't meet the upper weight limit before you are using a bigger seat they'll ride in through toddlerhood. Plus, even the lightest car seat will feel like it weighs a ton once you have a baby in it.

A Stroller

Two features matter most when it comes to strollers. Make sure it (1) works with your car seat and (2) is easy to fold and store. My favorite strollers have three important features: they can be used for a long time, they are easy to maneuver, and they are easy to collapse and store with a baby in tow. Just remember that you never want to run with a baby in a stroller until he is six months old, *even if* the stroller is advertised as a jogging stroller to avoid serious neck and head injuries.

Technology

Diapers, cleaning products, baby toys: they can all be purchased online and delivered to your home for a small fee. Have a friend set up an online meal calendar so that friends can bring warm food to nourish your family. This is the time to take advantage of a few modern conveniences. Really, you have more important things to do than drive around town, like sleep and bond with your baby.

Breast Pump and Accessories

Oh man, we have a lot to talk about here. When it comes to babies, there is a ton of junk you *do not need*. But when it comes to breastfeeding, more is more.

SETTING UP YOUR BREASTFEEDING GEAR

One of the biggest mistakes I see moms-to-be make is not to have their breastfeeding gear (breast pump and its coordinating parts) all set up before they have their baby. Yes, you can do it afterward, but if feeding is not going well and you need to use it, the last thing you want to do is spend time messing around with sanitizing pump equipment.

It is important for the breast pump to be a "double-electric" pump, which means it can pull from both of your breasts at the same time, it is strong enough to get the milk out, and it has some type of electric motor that makes it strong enough to get the milk out.

It also needs to work with a breast pump system, which means it's compatible with bottles for feeding, bottles for storing milk, cleaning supplies, cooler bags, freezer bags, and so on. You want all of this to work seamlessly together so you don't waste your priceless time jerry-rigging a ton of junk together.

One hidden consideration? It needs to have easy-to-find replacement parts. Most of the major brands out there should qualify. If it's not on Amazon or at Target, you'll be frantic when you really need a pump accessory and you just can't find one.

Most importantly—and this is not emphasized enough—you need something that is going to be *portable*. When I had my first daughter, I had this huge pump that needed to be plugged into a wall at all times to work. I quickly switched over to one that had extreme portability. (Note: for some moms with production issues, the strength of the pump is the most important factor, making other considerations seem frivolous. Follow your pediatrician's and lactation consultant's advice.)

Whichever setup you choose, most important is that you set it up and have it all sterilized *before* you have the baby. This is an awesome task to assign to a partner, but obviously, you'll be using it, so make sure you have a working knowledge of the pump yourself.

SETTING UP YOUR BREASTFEEDING SPACE

Consider, when buying your baby gear, where you will feed your baby. On the couch? In a rocking chair? Make sure that wherever you choose allows you to have 90-degree angles at your hips and your knees when you are feeding and has a wide enough space so that you can accommodate you, your baby, and a breastfeeding pillow when you are starting out. A lot of the fancy nursery chairs are too narrow to do that. Bring the feeding pillow to the store when you are trying to find a nursing chair. Don't forget about the furniture you already have in your house, too—the couch can sometimes be your best option. Often a step-stool at your feet can allow you to get in the right 90-90 positioning as well.

CHOOSING A FEEDING PILLOW

In the first few weeks to months, your baby will be small and you will not be used to breastfeeding. A breastfeeding pillow can be extremely helpful in positioning your baby so that you are more upright and are not leaning over your baby, which will help you to avoid neck and back strain, can help with flow issues, and, generally, will make life easier.

There are a number of different options, but the two most popular are the My Brest Friend pillow and the Boppy pillow. The lactation specialists at my office (and I) like the My Brest Friend pillow because it is more supportive for baby. It is, however, a little more bulky. The goal is to get your baby to nipple level. Sometimes you have to add a blanket underneath the pillow to raise it up. This is an item that you could easily borrow from a friend, because the cover is washable. If you have friends with both, try them both out.

WHEN TO USE A BOTTLE

Most experts agree that at about three to four weeks of age, using a bottle once a day or every other day will not compromise breastfeeding success. Until then, use pumping to build up your supply, but wait on using bottles unless instructed to use them by your medical provider.

They'll have special techniques to help keep your baby from developing a preference for taking milk from a bottle instead of from a breast (like finger feeding, a supplemental nursing system, or a special bottle called a Haberman bottle, which can be used to reduce reliance on a bottle).

CHOOSE THE RIGHT NIPPLE SIZE

One tip I learned early on? Babies sometimes prefer the bottle because the milk flows out of it a lot faster than it does from the breast (depending on the breast). This can also lead to more spit-ups and tummy aches. You may need to experiment with which nipple size works best for your baby.

For my first little one, I found that if I used the "preemie" nipple, it made her much more comfortable. For my second, it didn't matter which nipple we used—she was happy just to have the milk however it came. Don't be afraid to go down a size on the nipple if you feel like you are having trouble with fast flow.

WORTH IT TO INVEST

Insurance will often pay for a pump for moms, but look at the options they give you. You may need to upgrade to one that fits your needs so that you actually have one that will work for you. It's an investment, but if I were choosing between a spendy crib and a spendy breast pump, I would *always* choose the breast pump. It's not quite as fun to look at, but it will make your life significantly easier.

USING A HAND PUMP

A hand pump is a nonelectric device you can use to quickly pump off a small amount of milk without having to set up your whole pump system. It's awesome for a number of uses.

Overactive Letdown

If your first letdown sends your milk spraying all over your little one's face and looks like a torrential downpour, or your baby seems to have a hard time handling the flow, you may have overactive letdown. Check with a lactation specialist to see if this is true for you.

One trick I've learned is to attach the hand pump (again, having this sterilized before you have the baby is an excellent idea) and use it to get the first few letdowns' worth of milk so that you're not so completely full of milk when baby starts to eat and it is more comfortable for both of you.

Engorgement

In the first few days, it can be tough for baby to latch because your breasts are so large and the tissue is so tense. Sometimes a hand pump will help. Occasionally, you need your full-on double electric breast pump for this, but it can often be easier to whip out the hand pump and pump off a few ounces to make it easier for both of you.

When You Are Trying to Wean

Oftentimes, when you are weaning your baby, you'll have a bit of engorgement because your body is confused. Particularly if you have been nursing your baby for a long time, your body will automatically be ready to feed your baby at a session time you may have decided to cut out.

This is especially true in the morning. Although you don't want to give your body the full message "Yes! This body is still open for business!" you do want to relieve some of the discomfort from weaning engorgement. A hand pump can be great for this. A double-electric pump can also work, but it takes longer to set up in the middle of the night or in the morning, for example.

The great news is that a hand pump is pretty cheap compared to the cost of a double-electric breast pump; a hand pump will typically set you back eighteen to thirty-four dollars. It does *not* replace the double-electric pump, though. If you are trying to maintain your milk supply, only a baby sucking at your breast or using a double-electric pump will do the trick, because both create significantly more sustained suction for a longer period of time.

Two of my current favorites are the Medela Harmony Manual Breast Pump and the Haakaa. The great thing about the Medela is that, obviously, it works with the rest of your breast pump system. Several other companies make similar products that integrate with their respective bottles and pump parts. The downside is that you have to manually pump the breast to get the milk flowing. With the Haakaa, you attach the pump onto your breast (you can even attach it to your opposite breast when you are nursing to catch the extra milk), and once it starts working, you don't have to do anything—it's hands-free. The downside to the Haakaa is that once a baby gets wiggly, she can knock it off your breast, sending milk everywhere.

WHAT TO DO ABOUT ALL THOSE PRESENTS

We've talked about the top ten things you really need for your newborn. But what about all those presents you'll receive? Just between us, you probably don't need or want all of them. The tricky part is, you often won't know if you need them until you reach that stage. If something is for sure not your style, return it right away—you don't want extra junk to organize. If you're not sure and it's something the store always has in stock, take it back and get a gift card. Babies cost a lot to take care of—having extra cash later on to buy the things you really want (or need) can be a lifesaver.

SIMPLIFYING YOUR NEWBORN GEAR EXPERIENCE

You know the feeling when you go on vacation and you overpack? The way your bag gets heavier and heavier the longer you lug it through the airport, into the rental car, and through the resort lobby?

That's how it feels (times ten) when you fill your house with too much baby gear. The inevitable kid chaos just multiplies with the more stuff you purchase. Your outings feel more burdensome, your house feels more cluttered, and experiences that should be very straightforward (like going out to lunch for burgers and fries) suddenly feel very complicated. Keep it simple, and you'll be more sane.

4

FINDING A PEDIATRICIAN

She was about five months into the whole parenthood thing when she began to crumble. Every day, she woke with the hope that her little bundle of joy would decide that night (even if just for one night) to "sleep like a baby." And every night, she ended up rocking him back and forth for hours or shushing him loudly to the rhythm of the white noise machine. Five months.

She found me through my practice's website and a friend's referral right around that time. She said she hadn't really thought much about who her baby's doctor would be before he actually arrived, but when things got tough, she realized all of her Google searches weren't leading to any real answers. When she came to see me for the first time, exhausted and ready to quit, I could tell that she was fresh out of hope.

I've known that mom now for almost six years. She has a funny, handsome kindergartener who sleeps every night in his own bed *all night long*. We're a good team, she and I. And she'll tell anyone who will listen, "It really matters who helps you along in the beginning."

Many pediatricians will offer a complimentary prenatal visit where they meet with you to talk about the specifics of their practice. Call potential providers to find out.

Finding a pediatrician can seem like a daunting task, but five main features tend to set stellar pediatric specialists apart from their peers. You can refer to the checklist items I've outlined at the end of this chapter as well. Those factors are important, but not as important as these five.

THE OFFICE PRACTICE

Look at the specifics of the practice in which you're interested. Do they have weekend or holiday hours? Are there nurses available to answer questions you may have (even if those questions come in the middle of the night)? What are the extra services they have—is there a lactation specialist, a dietitian? Behavioral health providers? How up to date is their technological setup? Can you make your own appointments? Can you email your provider?

EXPERIENCE AND CERTIFICATIONS

Look at the experience and board-certification status of the person you are choosing. All pediatricians who are certified to practice medicine by the American Board of Pediatrics have to pass examinations on a regular basis, keep up to date on continuing medical education, and graduate from an accredited four-year medical school program and three-year pediatric residency program.

YOUR LEVEL OF NEED

Make sure that the person you choose can accommodate your level of attention and need. Some parents are pretty laid back. They obviously care about their babies and want the best for them, but they generally take the information medical professionals give them at face value and don't need extended conversations with their providers about each decision they make. Others need more explanation, time, and information to feel heard and confident. Knowing what basket you fall into, or if you are somewhere in the middle, is extremely important. Just like you can't and wouldn't want to change your personality, neither can the human being from whom you are seeking care.

THE "LET'S GET REAL" FACTOR

In my opinion, finding a doctor who can look you in the eye and tell you his honest opinion, giving you real, practical information you can really use, is invaluable.

Especially as a new parent, you're going to have a lot of questions. Some of them will have black-and-white answers. "Should I take my three-day-old newborn camping?" Absolutely not. Most of them, though, will be in a gray zone. You want someone who can present the pros and cons of your choices clearly and with confidence so you can make the best decisions possible.

WHOLE HEALTH

Make sure the practice and person you choose focus not only on physical health but also on social, developmental, and mental health. We know that healthy kids not only grow in height and weight appropriately but also reach their full potential when it comes to behavior and relationships.

In our clinic, we have on-site psychologists and a dietitian who team with us to maximize health holistically. We partner with other pediatricians in the community to compare clinic strategies and maintain the highest level of quality possible. Every three months, we review current research and recommendations from experts in the pediatric field.

Our pediatricians also meet regularly to discuss behavioral health and resilience with our mental health specialists so that we are current on best care practices for our patients. We work to be integrated, providing the best care possible in a way that fits the unique needs of our patients and their caregivers. Staff, parents and providers all give input as we design workflows and projects.

Will choosing the "right" pediatrician solve all of your parenting woes and make your parenting journey pain-free? Of course not. Is there a perfect pediatrician or pediatrics practice out there? No way. (I'll fully admit to that as a member of this specialty area.) Can you move through your early parenting experience knowing you have the support and knowledge base of someone who knows a ton about your child's health and cares a ton about your mommyhood success? Yes.

Pediatrician Interview Checklist

AAP BOARD-CERTIFIED PEDIATRICIAN STATUS

AVAILABILITY AND ACCESS
– Phones
– Email
– Office Hours
– Advice Nurses
– Website
– Urgent/Same-Day Appointments

CLINIC REPUTATION
– Longevity of Practice
– Unique Features: Dietitian, Psychologists, Lactation Specialists

EXPERIENCE
– Years in Practice
– Training Background/Special Areas of Expertise

HOSPITAL PRIVILEGES AND AFFILIATIONS
– Do they come see babies in the hospital?
– Local ER Recommendations

BOOK AND WEBSITE RECOMMENDATIONS

WHAT TO EXPECT AT CLINIC
– Appointments in First 3 Days
– Appointments in First 2 Weeks

Where do you find an amazing pediatric provider? Querying friends is an excellent place to start. Your obstetrician and local hospital can also serve as referral sources. If you're feeling stuck, ask your health insurance company—it will have a list of in-network pediatricians taking new patients in your area. Once you've identified a few top contenders, go online to check out candidates' websites, then set up a prenatal interview to see which expert is the best fit.

5

TAKING CARE OF YOURSELF AND YOUR PARTNER

Bitter, sad, disappointed. Pining away for something else. For what? For some other version of this life. For more of the parts of life I actually enjoy. For space to breathe. For space to enjoy. For freedom. But really? Before having kids, it was restlessness for the next step of life that kept me whining. Now it's a longing for time to be mine when I am off of work, to not be jealous when dad gets time away from us. For all of it. I want time to be by myself, but once I have it, I squander it. I'm so tired. I miss my freedom. I miss myself. It's unsustainable.

So many new parents I meet are in this boat, usually after the shine wears off at about the two-week or one-month mark postpartum. Adrenaline can only take you so far, and when that dissipates, it can be rough.

So many new moms are feeling desperate, and trapped, and really broken. Not only when it comes to their relationship with their partner but also when it comes to their sense of self. Having a baby is a huge transition—one for which we don't prepare moms well. It will inevitably change your relationship with your partner, and it will definitely challenge the self-directed, freedom-loving paradigm you know now, especially if you are a working mom-to-be and are climbing the corporate ladder. It's stressful to be a new mom, to say the absolute least.

Considering these issues before baby comes can help to ease the transition.

SOOTHER-IN-CHIEF

Expect your partner to be the soother-in chief. Count on him or her to be the expert on the soothing techniques we'll talk about in the up-coming chapters. If you are breastfeeding, you have a full-time job that requires rest, fluids, and patience to learn and perfect. You are the feeder-in-chief. You'll do your fair share of soothing as a function of that job. But your partner should take the lead on soothing so you can accomplish your main mission. If you are single parenting, gather trusted friends or family members around you to help calm and hold your baby early on.

GIVE IT SOME TIME

Understand that if your partner takes longer than you do to bond with your baby, it will come in due time.

My husband was always loving and in love with our daughter. He played with her and cuddled her every day in her first weeks. But just this month, he told me, "It was when she started laughing and reacting to me that I felt connected to her. That's when we bonded."

Looking back now, it's true. About a month into her life, he started asking me to send him pictures when he was at work and I was home with her. He started being sad when she was already asleep for the night by the time he got home and he couldn't participate in her bed-time routine. He missed her, and he didn't just love her now; he liked her, too! If you give your partner that chief soothing job, this will come faster.

YOU'RE NOT A MAGICIAN

Accept that you are not a magician and cannot develop a mom's intu-ition overnight. You need your partner's help, and (sometimes, believe it or not) partners have valid ideas! My husband learned this relatively early, thank goodness, with some gentle coaching from experienced dads. When my baby was crying at six weeks old and I had fed, rocked, shushed, and swayed her for hours with no end in sight, I needed an-other set of hands to give me a break. Even more important, I needed someone to take over mentally and emotionally for a little while. Two problem solvers are better than one.

EMBRACE DIFFERENCES

Embrace the fact that you and your partner parent differently. You have probably always done a lot of things differently; your differences just haven't been quite so in-your-face as they soon will be. You'll be trying to team up and create consistency for little Lucy, and your ideas about the best way to do that will be different some (or most) of the time. You may like different bottles; you may think certain toys are better than others. You may even have a different way of discussing which bottles or toys are the best!

For example, I'm a talker. I could hash out my thoughts about child-rearing verbally all day long. My husband *hates* doing that. He would rather think on his own about it, then have a short session where we try to problem-solve. I save the hashing out for my girlfriends (and my pediatrician), and I keep it short and sweet with hubby.

STRENGTHS AND WEAKNESSES

Parenting is a balance of tasks and responsibilities, and one partner may have more skills or patience for some of them. My spouse is wonderful at taking the reins with our toddler. He can make a three-course dinner with grace. He can hold and change the baby deftly during the day. But at night, especially once he went back to work, asking him to fully participate on an equal basis was like asking a slumbering bear to rouse himself from his cave in the middle of winter.

The choices I felt I had at the beginning? Yell at him (over and over) to please wake up *or* do it all myself. Both made me resentful, to be honest. Instead, I settled on a more strengths-based plan: if he could just get her out of the bassinet and change her the first few times she woke (plus obviously stay up and problem solve with me when we had a rough night), I would handle the rest of the night shift. In the day, he could do a little more baby-holding while I rested and nursed.

Why did it take me until my second child arrived to realize this was a more workable and, in the end, satisfying plan? Because the first time around, I was way too focused on precise equality and task-sharing, not considering that he would happily take the lead during the day if I would just let the man sleep a little more at night.

Instead of criticizing or comparing contributions, figure out your partner's parenting superpowers. All of us bring amazing things to our parenting partnerships. I see all kinds of parents in clinic—analytical types asking tons of specific questions, the research-focused contingent searching for the evidence behind pediatric recommendations, laid-back parents letting the stresses of early parenting easily roll off their backs. We all have something we bring to the table. Your partner may be great at problem-solving sleep issues while you are the baby bath master. If you divide and conquer according to the things you're naturally good at, you'll be a stronger team.

GET DAD INVOLVED FROM THE BEGINNING

If you have a male partner, consider this:

I know some amazing dads. My husband is one of them. He cares so much about teaching my kids about their worlds. He's great at getting them excited about cooking and sports and gardening. He gets an A+ in my book (most days).

But the day my daughter came home, when he first earned his dad badge, he said he felt unprepared. Sure, we'd both been present at our birthing class and we both learned how to swaddle an infant. Looking back, though, he said he felt like he didn't know what to expect when it came to normal baby behavior and definitely didn't feel ready to take the lead on newborn care. I'm sure it didn't help that his wife was a pediatrician. Still, the more dads I meet, the more I find so many feel the same way.

I feel kind of bad for modern-day dads like the one who lives in my house. I mean, not as bad as I feel for modern-day moms. But I do feel bad. It seems like, when we empowered women to be just as fierce in the workplace as at home, forever changing modern-day motherhood, we forgot about educating men on how to change their perspective on modern-day fatherhood. We figured they would just adjust without any effort or preparation, magically skilled and knowledgeable in all things baby. Add in the Mr. Mom monikers and the media depictions of helpless dads fumbling through parenting—it's a not a surprise a lot of dads I see aren't sure exactly where they fit into the new parenting paradigm.

How do we include dads in the early baby care process? How do we, as mothers-to-be, encourage and empower them to be equal players as we parent our young children? I say, start here:

Get Educated Together

How does someone become an expert in any field? They study. If, as a mom, you are the only one in your family studying up on babies before or after your infant arrives, you're going to be the only one who knows anything. And, that means, you'll be the only one who feels confident enough to take charge.

Everyone learns in different ways. If you learn best by reading, your partner may learn best by attending a class. Or, he may learn best by talking with other dads who have been through the newborn dog days. It probably won't work to force your partner to learn the exact same way you do, but it will work to expect that both of you have a working knowledge of common baby issues, newborn care basics and proven calming techniques so you can problem-solve from the same educated perspective.

Take a Giant Step Back

It's annoying to have someone looking over your shoulder, micromanaging your every move. If you've ever had a super-controlling boss or are the child of a nitpicky parent, you know the feeling. When someone doesn't trust us or tries to manage us, it makes us feel resentful and irritated. We sometimes even lose our organic interest in the topic and stop putting our best effort into it.

That's what happens when we don't allow our partners to play an equal role in taking care of our children. We kind of sabotage our hope of true co-parenting. Instead, be conscious about how to empower your other half to be the parenting boss more often. That might mean actually leaving the house so he or she has the space to parent without your eagle eyes. It definitely will mean holding your tongue (or sighs or eye rolls or judgment) if your partner is not doing things exactly how you would do it. If you both get educated together, you can be equal "experts" and this won't be so hard.

Give Some Respect

Dads are not complete duds in the baby care department, despite how most TV shows and movies depict them. Seriously, the next time you watch any sitcom with a dad character, look out for all the clueless parent references they make, especially if the child is under three years old. Sometimes, we carry that same attitude toward our partners in real life. We act like, if our partners didn't birth our babies, they can't ever be bonafide baby whisperers.

The truth is, if we don't allow dads the space to be amazing family contributors, not just as winners at the office but also as dust-mop wielding, dinner-preparing, diaper-changing Jedis, we miss out on a ton of help and on a ton of balance in our lives.

LEARN TO SAY SORRY

You are going through one of the most significant changes in your life. So is your partner. There will be times you will implode or explode from the stress of that transition. At times like these, figure out if there is something to be learned or if the pot of water just got a little too hot and boiled over.

When my daughter was nine months old, we were driving home from a holiday gathering out of town and there was a huge traffic jam that set my daughter's bedtime back an hour and left her screaming in her car seat while we waited fifteen minutes to reach the exit so that we could safely pull over, adding even more time to the trip. It really wasn't a big deal, but because I was on day three of sleep training and I knew it would be harder for her to fall asleep at home since she was so overtired, it set me off.

Needless to say, I had to apologize to my husband later that night for convicting him of choosing the "wrong way home" and "ruining sleep training." Of course, it was not his fault. In fact, it had nothing to do with him. I was just aggravated.

GET TO THE CORE ISSUE

Most of the time, arguments in the early parenting days will be a combination of fear (that something will happen to your baby, that you will never be "you" again, that your baby isn't as advanced as other babies), frustration, and fatigue. It makes sense to develop a plan for self-care and for your relationship ahead of time so you're not both caught off-guard when things seem a little rocky. Having a new baby can be rough on relationships when you're first starting out, but it can also be an awesome opportunity to build teamwork, to clock memorable moments, and to appreciate what the other person brings to the table when it comes to your kids.

GET HELP IN WAYS THAT ARE ACTUALLY HELPFUL

People always tell you when you have a new baby to get a lot of help. Take breaks, take turns with your partner, let others cook and clean for you, they say. Great advice, except that it often means, in the end, a house full of well-meaning people giving unsolicited advice and observations for about three weeks, while you hold a screaming baby and try not to lose it completely. I see the same with many of the new moms who come to me in clinic.

A potentially better plan? Let family and friends come in smaller spurts. Order take-out instead of having people cook every meal for you, or, sometimes, have them just drop it off and then go home.

Meaningful help might come from sources that seem less traditional, like a doula or a caregiver. We relied pretty heavily on our nanny when we had our second baby. She was someone I knew would be respectful of our family process, would provide continuity for our eldest, and would not stress out easily. It's not that your loved ones are not important; it's that sometimes there is an extra layer of complexity to their constant involvement early on.

SET SOME BOUNDARIES

You're an extrovert? It will make you depressed not to have a posse around you at all times? Great. Let 'em help. But, if not, let the newborn period be your first lesson in exercising parenting boundaries: doing what will work the best for you and your family, even if it doesn't please every single person you know.

PRIORITIZE YOURSELF

I remember a mom friend telling me she had booked a day of massages and pedicures for herself a month after her second daughter arrived, and I felt slightly annoyed. She said she needed it. Really? What a seemingly selfish thing to do. But, in reality, she was doing herself and her family a huge favor. Taking small chunks of time for yourself as early on as possible is one of the best ways to keep yourself from feeling trapped as a new parent.

MAKE A SELF-CARE PLAN

Self-care is not about self-indulgence, it's about self-preservation.
—Audrey Lorde

The reality is, the only way to take the best care of your family is to make sure you're taking time to take care of yourself. Can you push through and be a mommy martyr for the next eighteen years? Sure. Will it leave you resentful and angry? Most definitely.

Even though self-help is necessary, it's helpful to remember one simple principle: *you cannot have it all as a new mom.*

I know the media tells you otherwise. I know it seems like you *should* be having it all. But look at your life. Do you now? Even when you've tried your best at it? Even without kids? I didn't.

I could never look exactly the way I wanted *and* be the best at my job *and* always have a hopping social calendar *and* travel the world *and* have tons of money in the bank *and* be peaceful and happy all the time at the same time. Anyone who tries to sell you otherwise is selling you lies.

You do, though, have time for the top three priorities in your life. And if you choose things that really do fit your needs (as opposed to what other people want you to do), you will have more space for the

34

extras.

My friend Christie is a business exec coach. She spends all day guiding leaders personally and professionally as they make million-dollar decisions. One night, discussing life at a bar, she took a cocktail napkin and wrote out the major categories of life—kids, spouse, work, exercise, friendships, hobbies, homemaking, travel/experiences, and appearance. For clarification, exercise to me meant releasing endorphins, stress reduction, and meditation, whereas appearance included everything that goes into looking put-together (including exercise for the purpose of having a good appearance).

She wrote them in random order, then asked me to rank them in order in the left-hand column of a blank page based on what I, in an ideal world, would spend the most time doing. "Rank them as a private, honest list, not based at all on what other people would think is the right way to rank them," she said.

I called it my Ideal List:

1. Exercise/stress reduction
2. Kids
3. Travel/experiences
4. Hobbies (including writing and reading)
5. Partner
6. Friendships
7. Homemaking (tasks like laundry and dishes)
8. Appearance
9. Work

In the next column, she asked me to rank what I actually think I spend my time on.

Here was my Reality List:

1. Work
2. Homemaking
3. Kids
4. Hobbies
5. Partner
6. Appearance

7. Friendships
8. Exercise/stress reduction
9. Travel/experiences

Then, she told me to compare them.

Scary Comparison	
Ideal	Reality
1. Exercise	1. Work
2. Kids	2. Homemaking
3. Travel	3. Kids
4. Hobbies	4. Hobbies
5. Partner	5. Partner
6. Friendships	6. Appearance
7. Homemaking	7. Friendships
8. Appearance	8. Exercise
9. Work	9. Travel

Look at the striking comparison between what my ideal life looked like and what my actual life looked like. This exercise is what convinced me to make a change in my life. Also, notice that while my kids were really high on the list, they were not first. That's okay. In fact, it's probably more healthy. Because, in the end, my kids are going to grow up and do their own thing (yours will, too, by the way). My husband was also not first. That's okay, too. It's important we have separate interests and desires, which we can only build if we spend some time doing things separately.

You might be thinking, "I'm going to have to work!" That is true for me, too. That's how I pay for the stinking music classes and nanny and quality food I want to provide for my kids in the first place. It's how my daughter goes to that fun preschool the nanny drops her off at. It's how we make sure we get to live in the house we do. There is not going to be some overhaul of my life that allows me to live work-free and spend all day sipping lattes while I supervise my child.

Also, you might have a different top three than I do, and that is totally fine. My husband is a huge extrovert. I had him make this list, and his was in a completely different order. No problem. That's the beauty of it.

I'm not saying don't go to work, don't figure out a way to get your house clean once your newborn arrives, but, like my friend says, "Work is like a parasite. It will leach out of you as much as you will give to it."

Same with housecleaning, and coordinating eighty million schedules. Of course, we have to do some of that to keep things running smoothly, but we can't let them suck the life out of us. The rest of the things on the list you'll have to consider like gravy or a cherry on top if you can get to them, at least in the early weeks and months of motherhood. Sprinkle your life with the things lower down on the list.

Sounds good to get your priorities in line from the get-go, right? But it takes a little preplanning to make it happen. I learned early on that, to do all I do, I have to automate and delegate.

AUTOMATE AND DELEGATE

Here is a simple truth: you are not the only person who can take care of your home, your kids, your bills, or your calendar. There is a ton out there about mental overload and what it is doing, particularly to women, to have constant running lists of to-dos in our minds all day long.

I'm going to walk you through the things I've delegated that have really changed my life. Of course, everyone is in a different position in terms of her budget. I'm not trying to make you go into debt. But, if it is at all possible, follow my lead so you're not drowning in chores.

Hire a House Cleaner

Get someone, even if it's a neighbor kid, to mow your lawn. Even the National Academy of Sciences agrees with me on this one. *The New York Times* and *Travel and Leisure* both recently published articles about the science-backed advantage of letting others do some of your dirty work.

I'm not sure what took me so long to get a house cleaner. But I will say this: my family consistently insinuates that it is not my best skill, so I should have known I was spinning my wheels when I tried over and over to clean like a pro. Hiring a house cleaner did two bonus things for me: it forced me to organize my house the night before she comes (put away all the clothes, pick up around the house), and it made me feel extremely calm as I stopped looking around my house every minute wishing it was more together as I tried to corral two small children.

Automate

What could a computer be doing for you? You've got to ask yourself this question in all areas of your life.

First, set up a meal service program. That American Academy of Sciences study on getting in a house cleaner? It also recommended ordering take-out.

A healthier and less costly solution? Prepackaged meal kits like Hello Fresh and Sunbasket. Pay attention to salt content and the actual amounts of fruits and vegetables (not all are created equal). I'm a fan of Sunbasket because it's super plant-based and can be adjusted to vegetarian lifestyles, they have a family plan, and you can skip whenever you want. I have an app on my phone, and they send me reminders each week to pick meals. We use this service for three of our meals per week, make simple dinners like chicken with broccoli and a grain two times a week, and eat out/get take-out two nights a week.

Take Advantage of Technology

I use Amazon Prime for *everything*. Diapers, wipes, sippy cups, household items like paper towels, hand soap, and toilet paper: they all come from online ordering. I love places like Target like the next mom, but I do *not* want to drag my kids through that store every other week. I also do not want to spend my time in a grocery store for basics. It's fun to pick out something to add to our family meals or to get specialty items, but carrying around a list and hauling two little people around is a waste, in my book. Instead, I order groceries every week using Prime Now or Instacart and have them delivered to my home in two hours.

Get Smart about Bills

What bills do you not have on autopay? What monthly or weekly items do you constantly forget? Do you have a system to remind yourself of to-dos as they come up for you randomly?

Shop Online

Children's clothing is another area where it pays to use technology. I focus on quality basics that can be handed down kid to kid, when possible. I would rather spend a little more but only have to shop four times a year (with some fun, "let's get a special outfit" outings sprinkled in) than pay less per item and have it last less than a month. This is very budget-dependent but, especially if you have multiple kids and they are the same gender, buying quality over quantity makes a difference.

MULTITASK OR SIMPLIFY

Use the Car to Your Full Advantage

If you have a newborn and are nursing, this is one of the most important, time-saving tricks around. I used it with both my children. While parked (safety first!) in my car, I used a hands-free pumping bra to make my outings efficient. Inserting the breast shields into the bra and attaching my hands-free pump, I covered myself with a breastfeeding cover, turned that puppy on, and drove wherever I need to go. On the way to exercise class, on the way in between meetings, it made my car the perfect pumping station. And it was, obviously, hands-free.

I used a cooler pack and disposable cleaning wipes made specifically for breast pump parts for short trips when I didn't have access to a sink. Then I thoroughly washed and sterilized everything once I was home or at work.

Maximize Nap Time

Naps are a great time to rest. Yes, they can also be a time to get bills paid, do the dishes, and put away the laundry, but once your baby arrives and you're in the swing of things, take stock of how you feel at the end of nap times. My guess is, if you spend the whole time breathlessly taking care of tasks, you'll feel exhausted. Consider instead dividing out what you do during naps so that you complete one or two tasks (like paying bills and doing one load of laundry).

Then take some time to regroup and do something you want to do (even if it is scrolling through social media feeds) so you're not wishing you were doing that when your little one wakes up.

Same goes for planning. Set a planning day every week. My day is Wednesday. I spend Thursdays with my girls, so before that happens, I like to get all organized Wednesday nights. It's the night I figure out meals for the week, pay all the bills, do any online shopping I need to do, check my checking accounts, hash out details about upcoming events we have with my partner, and look at the calendar.

Use Audiobooks and Podcasts

On days when I am not driving to and from activities I really want to do for myself (like on days I am driving to work or driving around running errands), I spend the time in the car listening to podcasts and audiobooks. I love reading paper books, but I just know I would never have the time to get to everything I've had on my "meaning to" list if I relied on my evenings and weekends. That was especially true when I was a new mom. The car was a place where, when I was by myself, I knew I could get a lot done by listening.

Get Organized

Lastly, find the system of organization that fits you. I still use an old-school notebook to write out my goals and to project plan, but I need my phone calendar to keep organized. If something is not in my calendar, it does not exist.

FINDING A SELF-CARE RITUAL

A Plan That Works for You

When I was choosing an exercise program for myself postpartum, my friends and my husband talked a lot about running, Pilates, or joining a gym. Those can be *great* for some people. I have done a lot of running in the past, and it was amazing, but it wasn't the right thing for me this time around.

They also talked about working out first thing in the morning. "Get up really early, go work out, get ready, and then go straight to work," they said.

I tried that for a long time, feeling like that was the most responsible path to take, the way that would least inconvenience everyone else around me. But it didn't work for three reasons:

1. I never worked as hard as I would later in the day when I went to morning classes. I felt sorry for myself that I was up so early and didn't push myself because I was proud of myself just for showing up

2. I hardly ever actually went. I always found an excuse, namely, sleeping in as much as possible, but also kids waking up early needing my attention, work meetings, illness—you name it, I used it as an excuse.

3. I was exhausted by the time I finished exercising, getting ready for the day, and getting myself to my job. I'm sure you can guess how often I worked out. That's right: never. Nope. Self-care is just like birth control. The type of birth control that is best for you is the one you will actually use consistently. The type of self-care you choose is the kind that actually fits you and your desires and life.

Almost hilariously, now running and early-morning workouts are the mainstay of my exercise and self-care regimen. That's because I have children who sleep through the night consistently and I have a lot of evening work commitments. A different season in my life equals a different self-care approach.

A Schedule That Fits Your Life

As you develop a self-care plan, you'll also have to decide how much time you're willing or able to commit to on a weekly basis. I decided pretty early on that three days a week was a reasonable goal.

What is something you can do three days a week, almost every single week? Of course, you will have setbacks, but if you can commit to three times a week most weeks, it will be often enough that you stick with it and it will become a routine. If you can get to your activity more often, awesome, but three times a week is a great start.

I schedule my self-care this way:

1. One weekend morning

2. One weekday evening when my husband is with our kids

3. One weekday evening when a caretaker is with our kids

Everyday Moments

You might be thinking that leaving your newborn baby will be impossible three times a week. In the beginning, especially as a breastfeeding mom, self-care will likely come in more abbreviated, sporadic moments. It may be something small, like taking five minutes to listen to your favorite song with your eyes closed, getting a small treat (lattes are my vice), going outside, or simply taking ten big breaths. Or it may be bigger, like taking thirty minutes to an hour to read a book or going to the grocery store alone. Even now, on my four nondedicated self-care days, I make sure that I get at least five purposeful minutes to myself.

Pay Attention to Your Breathing

You'll have to breathe anyway. How will you do it? Will you hold your breath? Take small breaths over and over? Can you learn how to concentrate on your breathing a little more when you get stressed? Even the way you move air in or out will contribute to your sense of peace and mindfulness as a new mom.

Choose to Enjoy

I've talked about taking advantage of naps and time in the car, but sometimes it pays just to enjoy versus multitask. I make it a point *not* to listen to the news on the way home from work once I returned from my maternity leave. I used that time to turn on my music, turn it up loud, and enjoy it. I saved my news and podcast consumption for errands and my work commute.

At home, when my kids were asleep, we were intentional in the early days to watch a lot of comedies and to listen to a lot of frivolously entertaining audiobooks.

Take a Break

Take the time—even if it's one or two minutes—to get your head right in the middle of the day. If you're at home, it might be in the shower when you get a second to relax or at a time when your baby is asleep. If you are returning to work, it might be a moment at lunch when you turn off your phone, shut down your computer, and take a second to yourself or with your colleagues.

What's Worth It

If there were a single activity worth time by yourself, exercise (if you choose the right activity) or mindful meditation would take the cake. Exercise can give you the chance to deepen your social connections, be mindful, work on your own physical fitness, and set goals for yourself. Meditation also checks many of those same boxes.

MAKING MOMMY FRIENDS

Motherhood was never meant to be attempted alone yet, in the United States, isolated mommying is a common approach. Even before we have children, we often make more connections on a daily basis via social media than we do face-to-face with our peers. But, when it comes to being a new mom, you do need an actual, in-person village. Support may come from close friends, other moms you meet along the way, or family members. Even if you're naturally private, this is a time you'll need the insight and experience others have to offer.

I'm not talking about "baby and me" or "toddler and me" classes, where you sit in a circle and talk about your fears and worries. If those are your thing, more power to you. They are really useful for some moms, and it's great if they work for you.

Personally (and I find this for most other moms I meet), I found as a new mom that I preferred finding activities to do with other moms that were actual activities (like hiking groups or baby music classes), because I wanted to find like-minded moms and do something fun at the same time.

GIVE YOUR PARTNER SPACE

Remember, your partner needs time to regroup, too! Don't be stingy with taking care of yourself or with allowing the other caregivers in your life the chance to do the same. Before the birth, brainstorm activities that will bring him or her joy postpartum, either with you or as an individual.

KEEP YOUR BRAIN ACTIVE

Experienced parents set up a plan for what to do with their time once baby arrives. They focus on keeping their brains active starting at week one.

I spent so much time postpartum as a new mom sitting and watching TV. Alone. With my baby sleeping on me. It sounds cute and it was, for a few days. But, in the end, it was a bad thing to be isolated and mindless for so long.

When baby number two came along, I made a commitment to turn off the TV and turn on background music instead. I made playlists so I could already have music on-command that inspired and relaxed or energized me. I set up some (very light) contract work to do for a local health organization during my maternity leave. Mental engagement that is not stressful and not baby related is so important for newbie moms, especially if they are used to being at work forty hours per week.

STORE MILK

As soon as your milk comes in, use it to your advantage. Store small amounts so you can get small breaks starting at week three to four. In the beginning, you will have way more milk than you will once you are back to work pumping. It won't derail your nursing efforts to pump some of that and put it in the freezer or refrigerator. Here's how to do it: feed your baby first, then pump a little off to store—maybe one or two times per day.

If you are having supply issues to begin with, *of course*, give whatever your baby needs to him first. Also, if you are having overproduction issues and your lactation specialist tells you to do block feeding, only pump off enough to handle discomfort issues. But if that is not you, get to freedom faster by pumping that milk and letting others do some feeding once your latch and feeding rhythm is set—at about three to four weeks.

Storage Guidelines for Freshly Expressed Breastmilk
(For Healthy Term Babies; Reference: www.BreastmilkGuidelines.com)

Room Temp	Cooler with 3 Frozen Ice Packs	Fridge	Freezer
4–6 Hours at 66–78° F (19–26 °C)	24 Hours at 59 °F (15 °C)	3–8 Days at 39 °F or lower (4 °C)	6–9 Months at 0–4 °F (−18–12 °C)

6

FINDING A CHILDCARE PROVIDER

So you want to find an amazing childcare provider? I get it. I did, too. Kind of desperately. Like, in an "I am really trying to not bawl right now at the thought of leaving my precious baby in the arms of someone else, so if that someone else could be dreamlike, it would really help" kind of way. Choosing a care provider is one of the most important choices you make for your kids early on. The people your child are around strongly influence the way they see the world and the place they find within it.

I'm not going to mince words here. I have the world's best nanny. She has been with me for four years, through two very different infants, a remodel, and too many viruses to mention. You name it, she has done it. She makes my world go round, and she's gracious enough not to let it go to her head.

But I don't have the world's best nanny by accident. I have her by design. I had a specific plan when I set out to find her. So when parents ask me for recommendations on this topic, I have plenty of advice.

The most common question I get is, "Where do I find a great nanny/sitter?"

The answer: there are a ton of places to look for quality caregiver suggestions—online caregiver search sites, friends, family, coworkers, social media groups, even professional nanny companies. On the websites specifically designed for finding care, they'll make it pretty easy for you to go through all the steps—they'll allow you to create a profile, you create a job posting and filter through applicants, then set up in-person interviews. From there, you can do a paid trial where the caregiver watches your child for just an hour or so while you're still in the house so that you can make sure you feel comfortable.

Here's the secret, though: it's not about where; it's about how. It doesn't matter what site you use or what friend makes an initial suggestion. It matters what process you go through to attract, evaluate, and hire potential candidates.

Here are my top four strategies for finding someone amazing.

GET DETAILED

Be thorough and specific as you outline your needs. Make sure you've covered all of the things that really matter to you as you create your job description so that the standard of applicant is raised from the get-go and you don't attract people who aren't a good fit. This is my exact job post from four years ago:

My husband and I are currently pregnant with our first baby and are due with our little girl mid-October. I will have about three months off work and then will go back. We are looking for a great nanny to care for our little one at our home on the days I work. We need someone sporadically starting in October and consistently starting in January. In mid-October to mid-January, it would be for babysitting, to get to know us and her, so I can get a break some days and so I could fill in at my work some days if needed before I officially go back.

We could work out what would work for your schedule, but we don't have specific guaranteed hours in mind. Starting mid-January, it would be part time guaranteed two days per week (the days I am working, which are Tuesday and Friday) plus whatever works for both parties for extra babysitting/extra days etc. We're looking for someone who could for sure commit to working with us until our daughter is one but possibly for longer, depending on our needs plus your needs.

GET SERIOUS

Present yourself in a way that attracts the person you want working for you. Get a contract together so you look professional yourself. Delineate vacation and sick day expectations, salary, hours and household duties. Online childcare search sites such as care.com and sittercity.com will often have free downloadable templates you can use as a jumping off point. Refine your contract according to your individual needs.

PLAN AHEAD

My nanny told me that when she saw my job post, she was really impressed, because I posted it about three months before I had my baby. I didn't need regular care for six months from the time of the job posting. She said she loved that. (If you are about to have your baby and you are just now trying to find care, please don't freak out. All is not lost.)

"If you are a really serious nanny and you're looking for a transition, you don't just try to find a position two weeks ahead of time. You look four to six months ahead."

Similarly, if you are searching for childcare centers, expect high-demand sites will have long waiting lists. Start your search early if possible.

GET CHOOSY

Feel free to weed out those who don't quite measure up. This is your kid we're talking about. You want a caregiver you feel great about. Filter out applicants who don't present themselves well (by having spelling or grammatical errors), who don't have the experience you're looking for, or who don't fit your style. If you start your search early, you're more likely to allow enough time to find a good pool of applicants from which to choose.

Sometimes when you meet someone in-person, it becomes even more clear that she is right (or wrong) for you. Use your gut to make your final decision. Check references. When someone said, "I know this is a big deal and I can tell you without reservation that you will be so happy you chose her—she's like family at this point," I knew I'd found a winner.

GET REAL

Get real about the things that really matter to you in a caregiver. Of course, things like CPR-certified status are important to me, but the five characteristics that topped my list once I got past my check-boxed items were these.

Intuitive

I wanted someone who was intuitive and confident. In my experience, this only comes from real experience. As a pediatrician, once you've seen a hundred ear infections, you can spot one a mile away. The same hard-earned confidence goes for caregivers.

If someone has "over ten years' experience" on her résumé but you dig in and it means watching her younger siblings, it doesn't count as much as someone who has watched four families over the course of five to ten years, ranging in ages from infancy to fifteen years old. That person probably knows her stuff.

Trustworthy

I wanted someone who was trustworthy. When we had our in-person interview with our nanny, I told her I was looking for someone who could call me for anything but who felt comfortable in most situations so that she wouldn't need to unless there was a real emergency.

Turns out that was what our nanny was looking for, too. She told me that one of the main reasons she *chose us* was because she knew she wouldn't be micromanaged all day long on things she knew a lot about. She presented herself as a professional and expected to be treated in the same way. She, of course, defers to my direction if needed, but because she is so trustworthy and confident, I hardly ever feel the need to redirect.

Loving

I wanted someone who deeply loved my kids. I think sometimes this can be one of the most daunting aspects of this whole search, but the reality is, when you are searching for someone to care for your children on a regular basis, it matters that they are loved during that time (of course, in a way that keeps your kids safe and that has appropriate boundaries), not just "watched."

This takes a little bit of letting go. It means that your children will form a relationship with someone who is not you, that they might one day call your nanny "mom" on accident, that it may sometimes feel like they love your nanny (*gulp!*) more than they love you. I feel your pain. Your children might very well fall in love with their caregiver, and that would be the *best-case* scenario, in the end. When I finally put aside my pride and didn't let that sabotage my nanny-search efforts, I was more successful.

Knowledgeable

I wanted someone who had a solid understanding of child development. I knew that, eventually, my nanny would be the one to discipline my kids during the day. At first, it would be all roses and sunshine while they were cute and cuddly, but if I was in this for the long haul (which I was), there would come a time that she would be handling tantrums and time-outs. I wanted this to be second nature to her.

Let me be clear: this doesn't mean a caregiver has to take official courses in child development. It also doesn't necessarily mean that she can quote experts in the field of behavior management (can you?). It means that she can walk you through what she would do if a tricky situation came up with your child, with her explanation making you say, "Wow, I would never have thought to do that! That's a genius idea!"

A Good Fit

I wanted someone I actually liked. This is so important. You really have to make sure that the person you hire is someone you would be okay spending time with or, even better, would want to spend time with. She doesn't need to be your best friend, but odds are, you will develop a friendship with her as you share the responsibility of raising your kids together. If you are irritated by her half the time, the odds of this all working out will start to wear on you. Spend time in your interview asking a bit about your potential employee so that you have a good sense of the person you are inviting into your home.

WHAT ABOUT DAY CARE?

In my book, quality childcare provides a safe space where kids can build deep, one-on-one connections with their caregivers and (important for all working parents) is a place where kids do not get sick all day, every day. The program or person also needs to provide the level of flexibility you need. Finally, you want the adults caring for your child to have the same parenting goals and values you do, backed by a working knowledge of the core principles of successful caregiving.

You don't want them to try too hard to focus on a set "curriculum" for children. Instead, you want them to provide opportunities for exposure to lots of books, music, one-on-one communication opportunities, and exploration. This could be in the care of a day care center, an in-home day care, a nanny, a nanny share, a friend, or a relative.

Good caregivers:

- Manage their expectations
- Understand child development
- Respond versus react
- Promote strengths and accept weaknesses
- Address their own issues
- Have the right priorities
- Focus on resilience
- Make time for themselves

They share these goals for your kids, giving care in a way that helps kids:

- Contribute to society
- Find contentment in their work and play
- Form healthy relationships
- Have resilience

My top picks are nannies, family members and in-home day cares for young kids. Once kids reach preschool age, the need for structure and social skill development outweighs the home care aspect. At that point, a mix of preschool and sitter/nanny is my top choice. Of course, budget comes into play, and traditional day care settings, as long as the caregivers are really quality, are a great option, too.

Like most things in life, what really matters when it comes to childcare is that you feel comfortable and confident with your choice. The exact location or setup matters less. Day cares and nannies can be great options, but just make sure you find quality caregivers who share your goals and values—that is most important.

Finding a nanny or caregiver can be stressful, but it's also really exciting. You're building your village, hiring the person who will be there for your kids alongside you, nurturing, guiding, and caring for the person or people you love best. Focus on finding experienced, quality providers. You'll find amazing people waiting in the wings to work with you.

Nanny Questionnaire

EXPERIENCE
— Number of families/ages of children
— Length of time with other families
— Specific experience with newborns

AVAILABILITY
— Hours of current availability
— Other commitments (school, other families, etc.)
— Upcoming vacation needs/anticipated time-off needs

HEALTH
— Vaccination status
— Smoking status

CERTIFICATIONS and EDUCATION
— CPR and first aid certification status
— Child development knowledge/experience
— Comfort level with health issues (fevers, colds, emergencies, special-needs children)

FAVORITE AGES and ACTIVITIES with KIDS
— Knowledge of local-area kid-friendly venues
— Favorite local parks, swimming pools, classes

HANDLING DIFFICULT SITUATIONS
— Describe a time a baby was crying uncontrollably and you had to figure out why.
— Describe a difficult situation you've had with a toddler and how you solved it.
— Describe an emergency you've had to deal with.

NEGATIVE OR POSITIVE PAST WORK EXPERIENCES
— Describe what went well or what was frustrating.
— Describe a "deal breaker" for you when finding a nanny position.

ADDITIONAL TASKS
— Open to light house cleaning/cooking?
— Able to transport kids via car/public transportation?

OTHER FAMILIES and HOBBIES
— Open to play dates with other children?
— Any special hobbies (art, music, other languages you would incorporate into childcare)?

SECTION II

WHEN BABY ARRIVES

7

IN THE HOSPITAL

I'm not sure when Pinterest became the go-to information source for moms-to-be. It has simplified creating checklists for all things in the pregnancy and birth preparation realm, that's for sure. There are checklists for what to bring to the hospital, for how to pack for post-partum needs, and for what to include in your birth plan (the most successful moms I meet have a very simple birth plan of "keeping mom and baby healthy and safe," by the way).

I think the cultural obsession we have with planning and control-ling the birth and postpartum period is rooted in fear. We're scared it will all go wrong. And we're a little bit right to be fearful—sometimes it does go wrong. But usually, it goes just fine, and the superficial checklist items we make sure we address before baby comes are defi-nitely not the deciding factors in our success. It will all be okay no matter what labor playlist you curate or which bathrobe you pack. It will work out no matter which newborn outfit you buy for the car ride home.

There are, though, factors that do play a role in helping you and your baby get off to the right start. The first is having a basic under-standing of how the hospital system works and who the main players are in your care. That way, you can self-advocate effectively. The sec-ond is an understanding of the normal hospital postpartum timeline, so you can prepare yourself for what will happen to most babies in the first hours to days.

In the hospital, nurses are the main people who take care of babies. They'll do all of the initial weighing, measuring, and monitoring. If you are in a traditional hospital setting, a pediatrics specialist—either someone who works for the hospital or who comes from an outside clinic—will also check on your baby to make sure everything is okay.

The nurses, though, are your main source of help with breastfeeding while you're there. Take advantage of their expertise and time to make sure you feel as confident as possible with your latch. It may feel like the doctor is never around. In fact, the nurses have 24-7 private line access to a pediatrics expert. They will call right away if they are concerned.

Following are common things that will happen to your baby when he is in the hospital (unless you refuse them).

Cardiac Screening

Several issues with a baby's heart can present in the first few hours, days, or weeks of her life. Most hospitals have instituted a screening protocol to catch most of these issues. It can't catch everything, but it can catch a lot. A tiny, painless sensor, called an oxygen saturation monitor, will be put on your baby. This will read how much oxygen is in your baby's blood, giving experts a great indicator of how her heart is doing.

Vitamin K

Vitamin K is a substance in the blood that helps it form clots. Clots are the little clumps of platelets that help keep your body from bleeding when it is not supposed to. For example, when you scrape your knee, your body forms a clot. Some people's bodies don't have enough of this substance and cannot form these important little clumps. It wouldn't be that big of a deal if we were just talking about scraped knees, but clots are important for preventing bleeds in the brain, the gut, everywhere in the body. It's very difficult to know at birth who has and does not have enough vitamin K, so all babies are given this in the hospital.

Erythromycin

When babies come through the birth canal, they are exposed to all of the germs sitting around in the vaginal canal. Though you may be 100 percent confident in your sexually transmitted infection (STI) status and, if you had prenatal care, would have had STI testing in pregnancy, erythromycin ointment is a gel that we put on babies' eyes to make sure that, in the very off-chance an infection was missed, that infection does not go to the baby's eyes and cause permanent damage.

Bilirubin Testing

Jaundice is the yellow color of skin that is a result of a product called bilirubin in the blood. Bilirubin has some antioxidant properties and is useful in small amounts to us, but when there is too much, it can cross what is called the *blood-brain barrier* and cause problems in the brain.

Jaundice can be caused by a variety of things, but in the early days, one of the main reasons a baby gets jaundiced is because he has dipped down too far in his weight and is dehydrated.

At twenty-four hours of life, all babies in the hospital have a bilirubin test. This helps the hospital see if they need to do anything to intervene if the level is really high. At the newborn nursery, special interventions called *phototherapy* can be used if the level of jaundice is too high, and your nurse and provider can work together to figure out the cause of the jaundice.

Hepatitis B Vaccine

Hepatitis B is a serious virus that can affect the liver and lead to permanent damage or cancer. Although many people think of hepatitis B as only affecting IV drug users or those with high-risk sexual behaviors, it is highly contagious for a baby when she comes through the birth canal as well. It also can be contracted via blood-to-blood contact (i.e., during diaper changes or if a baby needs her blood taken, which can happen often in the first few weeks of a baby's life).

The younger you are, the more likely you are to contract hepatitis B if you are exposed to it, and the more likely you are to have permanent, serious problems from it. In my practice, we recommend the hepatitis B vaccine before discharge from the hospital, and then baby gets boosters later on in infancy.

Newborn Screen

Newborn screening is a public health effort to catch treatable diseases early on in babies that could otherwise be devastating to them—things like cystic fibrosis, thyroid disease, and metabolic disorders (where babies can die suddenly because they can't process sugars or proteins correctly). All states in the United States have a newborn screening program.

Getting your baby tested involves a tiny heel prick—the blood is sent to the state and the screening program contacts you and your doctor right away if there is an issue. No news is good news for the newborn screening program. Generally, this test is done in the first few days of life, with a second test at two weeks old.

Hearing Screen

All babies have a hearing screen before they leave the hospital. Some babies have a little bit of fluid in their ears when they are first born and will fail the screen for that reason. The hospital will set up a repeat screen or will give you instructions on how to arrange the repeat before you leave the hospital. It's really important to follow up if there was any initial concern, because hearing deficits can impede language development significantly, and if we catch them early, we can intervene as soon as possible.

THE HOSPITAL TIMELINE

For a baby born via vaginal delivery, health insurance will often cover care in the hospital for two nights. If your baby were to be born at 10:30 pm, that would count as one night. If she were born at 1:30 pm that same day, it means the same. For C-sections, the general rule is three nights (check with your insurance—all plans are different).

In our setup, a doctor will come to the hospital to do an initial baby check within the first twenty-four hours after a baby is born—usually the morning after baby has been delivered. On that first visit, we'll review what happened during the delivery, talk with the nurses about any concerns they have, come into the hospital room to talk with you about any concerns you have, examine your baby (the nurses will have already done this, but we do our own look), and make a plan for the day.

The plan is not that complicated: it's generally rest, eat, get as much help as you can from your nurses, and focus on learning how to feed your baby. Your milk will usually not be in yet, but your baby will be getting tiny bits of fluid called colostrum, which has a *ton* of amazing benefits for your baby, such as antibodies and antioxidants.

Unless there are problems (like your baby needs extra attention for feeding problems, we have concerns about infection, or there are other worries), we'll come back to see the baby on the day she is ready to be discharged from the hospital to your home. On that exam day, we'll go over how to feed your baby (see a theme here?) and signs of infection to look for.

We'll also set up an appointment with your baby's doctor. This appointment date depends on how things are going. For second-time parents and for parents of babies where everything seems to be hunky-dory, we'll generally see you two to three days later. If we are concerned, we'll see you the next day in clinic.

MY #1 TIP

Stay in the hospital for the full amount of time your insurance allows, if possible. A lot of parents ask me if they can leave at the twenty-four-hour mark. If things are okay with baby, that is a possibility, but I encourage them not to. Here's why: besides the actual delivery, the *second* twenty-four hours of life are when babies tend to have issues.

THE DAY YOU GO HOME

When parents leave the hospital, I find that they fall into one of three groups: they don't worry enough, they worry too much, or they worry just the right amount. It's a Goldilocks' situation that is very hard to get right. Pro tip: even the experienced freak out a bit. I did with my first child, and I had been giving parents advice for years about how to have a new baby. That's normal. You have crazy hormones and you have never been responsible for another human being before.

Let's look at the two extreme groups so you can be as successful as possible.

Not Worried Enough

This is the scariest group for me, honestly. Why does it happen? You've been in the hospital; everyone has said that things seem to be going well; for those first twenty-four hours, your baby was super sleepy; and everything feels idyllic. You sleep a bunch in the hospital—maybe not all night, but more than you thought you would. You had a nurse waiting on you hand and foot to make sure it was all good. Some people carry that slightly lackadaisical attitude into their home environment.

They don't realize the most important rule about newborn babies: *they change rapidly*, and their needs are not always intuitive. What is true for their fluid needs right at birth is extremely different than their needs at two days, three days, and four days. Things ramp up really quickly (or at least should), and things that seem like no big deal (a small fever) can be a *really* big deal.

I once had a baby come in with her parents for her first baby check, and I asked them how it was going. They said, "Oh, amazing. Even better than we thought it would be. She slept for six hours last night, then barely ate, then slept again another six hours." That is *not normal*. That baby came in dehydrated and needed to have supplements. We barely kept her out of the hospital. Don't be that parent.

Too Worried

There really is no worrying too much when it comes to a newborn baby, but at some point, the balance tips and you don't get the sleep you need because of your anxiety, and your baby starts to pick up on the fact that you are uncomfortable.

The way to avoid this? Set yourself up with help from a lactation specialist or a doula so that you have a touchpoint along the way to reassure yourself and to guide you on the many little things that can go wrong. Ask for your doctor's appointment to be sooner once you are discharged. Stop searching the internet. Instead, look at or access reputable sources of information: doctors, nurses, lactation specialists, or quality books about newborns.

At our office, we also have a twenty-four-hour nurse line. I encourage new parents to call this as often as they need to. "You are not bothering us when you call us," I say. "You are the people we hope will call us when you are concerned."

The day you go home with your baby can be really awesome and a little terrifying. If you find yourself in the more terrified category, take a deep breath and think about the resources you have around you.

8

WHAT'S NORMAL, WHAT'S NOT

When I was in medical school, we had a large section on abnormal dermatologic findings, spread out over the course of months and integrated across various body system courses. When we learned about cancerous diseases, we also learned about the ways those problems manifest themselves in the skin.

In the beginning, someone in the class would inevitably start to freak out that he had some horrible illness whenever we learned about a new condition, convinced he should call his family and arrange for a memorial service on the spot.

He needed a reality check, which usually came from a visit with his own physician. Over time, though, we became more accustomed to recognizing normal and abnormal in our patients and in ourselves (that is the point of medical training, it turns out). We transformed into confident, knowledgeable experts who used our rational observation and decision-making skills to come to diagnostic conclusions.

The same transformation happens for most new parents over time. At first, everything they notice on their newborns seems like a life-threatening lesion. Each rash drives them on a daylong Google search. Slowly, over time, they learn what they should worry about and what is to be expected.

A parent's education starts at the hospital, but things are so chaotic and new there that it's really at the first doctor's visit that what's normal and what's not tends to sink in.

DOCTOR VISITS

Generally speaking, you will have an appointment with your pediatrician a few days after leaving the hospital (give or take, depending on your situation) and again at two weeks of age. Between those two appointments, visits in the first two weeks are determined by need. Here are the issues that tend to bring kids back in sooner (your doctor will let you know if she needs to see you for these).

WEIGHT LOSS

Before a mom's breastmilk comes in, a baby naturally loses a bit of weight. If your milk doesn't seem to be coming in, if your milk is in but your baby is still not gaining weight, or if your baby continues losing weight beyond what is considered "normal," we want to help the baby get on the right track.

Here's why this is super important in the first week: if a baby doesn't get enough fluid, she can become dehydrated, which can make her more jaundiced. Also, if she doesn't get enough fluid, her blood sugar can drop, which can make her more sleepy and not want to eat as much. She doesn't have a lot of reserves, so she can start to spiral down pretty quickly. On the other hand, if we can get her moving in the right direction, she can bounce back with the energy she needs to thrive.

JAUNDICE

That first week is prime time for a baby to get jaundiced. While almost every baby has a tiny bit of jaundice, which we call "physiologic jaundice," some babies get to a more dangerous jaundice zone and need more help (or at least monitoring). Very rarely, this means going back to the hospital, but often it does mean working on getting more hydration or, sometimes, doing a home jaundice treatment called a *bilirubin blanket*.

OTHER FEEDING ISSUES

I've brought families back into my office for issues with latching, for excessive spittiness, or *just because a parent is concerned*. It's worth it to express your needs to me, because I want you to get super comfy in your own skin as you start to parent.

SIGNS OF ILLNESS

When you and your newborn go to the doctor for the first time, we'll look closely for signs of infection and educate new parents about what to expect so they can catch illness right away. You should call your doctor about these concerns as soon as possible (remember: you are not a nuisance to your pediatrician). If you are worried, just call. Figuring out what you need to be worried about and what you don't need to be worried about is part of the learning process as you become a parent. Better safe than sorry.

Persistent Fast Breathing

It's never normal for a baby to breathe fast consistently (more than one breath per second) or to have what is commonly called *labored breathing* for a sustained amount of time. I often describe labored breathing to parents as sucking in at the ribs or the belly, flaring at the nose, or breathing hard like the baby just ran a marathon.

Fever 100.4°F (or 38°C) or Higher

You do not need to check your baby for a fever all day every day. But if your baby seems fussy and is warm, check his temp. When a newborn has a fever in the first month of life, it can signal a very serious infection in the blood, in the urine, or in the fluid surrounding the brain and spinal cord. Call your doctor's advice nurse for help with this, day or night.

Lethargy

Lethargy is a tough word because it means different things to different people. It doesn't just mean sleepy to medical professionals. To me, it means a baby is acting so out of it that you could poke him with a stick and he wouldn't care. If a newborn misses more than one feed, that could be a sign of lethargy.

Projectile Vomiting

This means the vomit literally makes an arc across the sky and hits someone or something. Spit-up that dribbles down the chin is not projectile vomiting.

Blood in Stool or Vomit

It's never normal to have blood in a newborn baby's vomit or stool (or persistent bleeding from anywhere, for that matter); this can signal a major issue in the digestive tract. Occasionally, if a mom's nipple cracks from nursing trauma, a baby can swallow a little bit of blood and fake us all out, but don't take any chances. If you see blood, call right away.

Cyanosis

Cyanosis is a gray or blue color around the lips. In a newborn baby, it can signal infection or heart disease, especially if it comes on with feeding. On the other hand, acrocyanosis, a purple/gray/blue discoloration of the hands and feet, can be a normal infant finding we attribute to an immature circulation system.

Sweating or Panting during Feeds

If a baby pants or sweats while feeding, we worry that its body is stressed and that eating pushes it over the edge, so to speak, taxing its basic metabolic functions.

Severe Fussiness

Most babies are fussy, with a peak around six to eight weeks of life, but we worry when babies are completely inconsolable for hours on end. That warrants a call or a trip to the doctor.

NORMAL FREAK-OUT FINDINGS

On the other hand, these are a bunch of common findings that tend to really freak parents out, even though they are completely normal.

Erythema Toxicum

This is a completely benign rash with a horrible name and a worrisome appearance: scattered little red dots with white centers. It tends to resolve on its own by one week of life.

Cross-Eyed Appearance

A baby's eye muscles are often not strong enough to keep her eyes aligned until a few months of age. It can be normal for a baby's eyes to cross until about two months old.

No Poop for Days

When a baby is just-out-of-the-womb-brand-new, pooping a lot means he is getting plenty of food. But after just a few weeks, breastfed newborns can go up to seven days without a stool (as long as it's mushy when it eventually does come out). A hard stool after that long without another bowel movement does warrant a call to your pediatrician, though.

Hiccups

Just like the rest of a baby's nervous system is extremely immature, so is the diaphragm. Some babies hiccup a *ton* in the first few weeks. Don't sweat it.

Congestion and Sneezing

Babies have been living in a water-filled environment for months when they're born—it's normal that they would need to clear out some of that fluid from the nasal passages. If babies have even more fluid after several weeks, though, that's something to check with a doctor about. It may mean they need to help you with positioning or with assessing for overactive letdown.

Periodic Breathing

It's okay if a newborn's breathing is not completely uniform. Babies will often have episodes when they breathe fast for a few seconds and then go back to their normal rhythm. If they have continuous fast breathing, it's worth it to reach out for help.

The "Mini-Period"

Lots of baby girls have a small amount of blood in the diaper at day four to five as their mothers' hormones (estrogen) leave their bodies. We call this a "mini-period." It may last for a few diapers before resolving, leaving dads and moms everywhere petrified. Large amounts of blood are never normal.

A Stinky Umbilical Cord

When the umbilical cord falls off of a baby, it can be kind of stinky. That's because it is a piece of rotting flesh! It's okay if there is a slight odor, but if there is extreme redness, swelling, or pus, parents should call the pediatrician right away—those are signs of potential infection.

Primitive Reflexes

Until babies are about three months old, they have what we call primitive reflexes (also known as startle movements). The most commonly recognized is the Moro reflex, where a baby puts its arms out to the side and jerkingly flutters them forward when she has the sensation of falling (like when being set on her back).

Slate Gray Patches

These are small areas of pigmented skin that can show up on the back or the buttocks. Occasionally, they are mistaken for bruises or can make parents concerned that they are dangerous lesions, but they are completely harmless. They are especially common on the skin of babies of color.

Dry Skin

When babies are first born, their skin can look dry and flaky after a few days of birth. They have been in water for a long time—it takes a while for the skin to adjust. This is not dangerous. Just let it be, and it will resolve on its own. You can use gentle products like Aquaphor Healing Ointment if the skin gets really dry and cracked in the creases of the ankles or wrists.

Babies don't need baths in the first few weeks of life. They just don't get that dirty. Obviously, clean their bottoms when they poop and spot clean if they get spit-up, but otherwise, letting a baby's skin acclimate in the first few weeks without a bath is better, especially for umbilical cord healing.

Once you do start giving baths, my favorite products are gentle cleansers like CeraVe Baby Wash and Shampoo. I love fancy, great-smelling, natural products just like the next mom, but they can often cause irritation. More basic options can help to reduce the chance of rashes and other problems down the road.

9

SETTING YOURSELF UP FOR BREASTFEEDING SUCCESS

You're there in the hospital, a new mom, just trying to get your feet wet with the whole baby-feeding thing. Well-wishers, relatives, hospital staff—they all have a ton of advice. And given the gravity of the situation—the sinking feeling that you are now responsible for another human being and that his safety depends solely on you—it's understandable that you would be a little overwhelmed.

There, in the sea of recommendations and guidelines, one crucial principle often gets missed. It's critical to early breastfeeding success. It's a simple rule that, with incredible fatigue and postpartum recovery issues, can be hard to concentrate on: babies need to eat.

On the surface, that may seem oversimplified. I mean, *of course* babies need to eat. You knew that already. But the specifics of what they need and when they need it can be a bit more complicated.

Believe it or not, the first few days of your baby's life have a huge impact on your breastfeeding success. No pressure, right? Actually, there is a ton you cannot control, so most important is to know the basics of what to do when it goes right and then more specifically what can go wrong so you can get help when you need it.

Watch Breastfeeding Videos

Watch videos about breastfeeding before you have your baby. The Stanford University Nursery site (www.med.stanford.edu/newborn) has a great series about breastfeeding basics. Watch how the moms position their babies, and learn about latching properly. It will give you a book-level knowledge of what to do.

Get Latch Advice

When you are in the hospital, ask for help latching your baby right away. If possible, choose a hospital with nurses who are lactation certified so you get professional help as soon as possible. The gold standard is to get your baby latched to breast within one hour of birth, setting both of you up for success. Ask your nurse at the hospital to position correctly. Ask for a lactation consultation if you have any concerns at all (this is pretty much every new mom I meet, so don't feel like you have to have major worries in this area to justify getting extra assistance).

Feed Really Frequently

In the first few days to weeks, babies need to have a feeding attempt at least every three hours. We call it "three hours start to start" in my office—that is, it should be no longer than three hours from the start of one feeding to the start of another. Babies will often want to feed way more often than that, which is great and perfectly okay, but at the very least, they need that every-three-hour cueing.

Why? Breastfeeding is a two-way feedback loop. The first feedback loop is for the mom: the more a baby's suckling stimulates the breast, the more milk the mom's body makes. The second feedback loop is for the baby: the more the baby eats, the more food it takes in, and the more alert and hydrated the baby will be, driving hunger and allowing the baby to regulate its own feeding needs over time.

You may have heard two things that contradict this advice, so let me address them both.

First, people talk all the time about the fact that babies should feed "on demand"—that they should drive their own hunger and can do so, that breastfeeding should be natural. That's totally true . . . eventually. But in the beginning, a baby needs help getting her system going. Breastfeeding *is* natural, but it's not usually easy in the beginning for a new baby or a new mom—both have to learn new skills and how to rev up the system.

Second, there's a lot of talk in prenatal classes about how a baby's stomach is really small at first and how he doesn't need much milk, about how he really only needs the tiny bits of colostrum in the first few days. That is absolutely true. Babies are often sleepy in the first twenty-four hours after they are born, and mom's milk hasn't come in yet; the system is set up so that there's a little grace period.

But here's the catch: that is the time to prime the pump(s) by nursing frequently so that the milk actually does come in and so that baby is alert enough at day three to four so he can take the milk mom starts making. In some cases, if that doesn't happen, blood sugar levels can drop, making babies lethargic and harder to feed. Babies can get dehydrated, contributing to jaundice (the yellow color that can develop in a baby's skin).

Learn Stimulation Techniques

Ask the nurses early on to teach you tricks to get your baby to continue being stimulated when on the breast for the first time. We use techniques like "the chicken wing" (moving the baby's arm gently in a small circle), tickling her feet, using a cool cloth, and removing clothing so that she is motivated to continue eating once she starts). Otherwise, the baby may burn energy on sucking without getting much back in return.

Understand Basic Biology

If you end up needing breastfeeding equipment like nipple shields, make sure that you do extra pumping to offset the decreased stimulation to your breasts. Also, make sure that once your milk comes in, you are what they call "fitted" for breast shields (the cones that attach to the pump). Our lactation specialist says that if your breast shields are not the right size, it's like walking around in shoes that are too big or too small.

Breastfeeding in the hospital can be hard because it's all so new. Once they go home, a lot of moms realize those hours clocked in the hospital were really the Golden Days—a time when they had tons of help and resources. Take full advantage of your time before you go home.

BREASTFEEDING TIMELINE

A basic understanding of the way breastfeeding usually progresses allows you to recognize when things aren't going quite as planned.

Breastfeeding Timeline			
	Days 1–2	Days 2–3	Days 4–5
Breastmilk	Colostrum Thick, Syrupy Yellow-Gold Nutrient Dense	Milk Comes in Thinner, Lighter Yellow, Higher Volume	Thin May Layer Skim Milk Appearance
Stomach Size and Capacity	Cherry 5–7 ml	Walnut 22–27 ml	Apricot 45–60 ml
Stool	1–2 Wet Greenish-Black Meconium Stool	5–6 Wet At Least 3 Dirty May Look Green/Mix of Dark Brown + Green	6+ Wet At Least 3 Dirty May Look Yellow, Seedy, Runny

Now, sometimes even more importantly, what can go wrong? Most people do not talk much about this. I think it is in the name of not making people panic, but the reality is that breastfeeding is really hard. A lot of moms tell me they wish that someone had actually been real with them about that.

I know I panicked a lot because I didn't consider these possible issues.

Difficult Latch

It can feel uncomfortable at first when most babies learn to nurse because their suction is stronger than anything your breasts have ever experienced. But if the pain is severe or persistent, you need to get help. If you have nurses or a lactation specialist help you in the hospital, having them help you assess latch is one of the most important things you can do. This is one of those things that is impossible to know until you are actually doing it—watching a video can help you to know the basics of latching, but it can't replace the real thing.

Excessive Weight Loss

If your baby isn't getting enough milk, she can lose too much weight. By about day 3 to day 4, your milk should be in. You'll start to see your baby really swallowing when she is eating, and you may see milk at the corner of her mouth. If that isn't happening, again, it means you need help.

We expect that babies will lose up to 10 percent of their birth weight in the first few days of life. But once mom's milk is well established, that weight loss corrects itself.

One of the major indicators of a normal progression is poop, which changes rapidly as mom's milk comes in.

POOP CHANGES IN THE FIRST WEEK

Getting familiar with the normal progression of stool changes in the first week can reassure you that feeding is going well or alert you to seek assistance.

Poop Changes in the First Week		
Day	**Number**	**Color**
1–2	1–2	Green-Black Meconium
2–3	3+	Mix Green/Brown
4–5	3+	Yellow, Seedy, Runny

Jaundice

If your baby looks yellow, it is a sign of something called jaundice. You can read more about this back in Chapter 7.

In the hospital, part of the standard of care is to check bilirubin at about twenty-four hours (or sooner, if needed), so you will get feedback from the professionals caring for your baby if this is an issue. Once you get home, though, paying attention to how yellow your baby's skin looks is really important. If you are worried, call for help.

Difficulty Handling Feeds

All babies have a very floppy connection between the feeding tube, or esophagus, and the stomach. This is called the *pylorus*. While for some babies, this connection valve can be too tight, causing something caused *pyloric stenosis* (a very serious condition that needs to be treated right away—projectile vomiting is the hallmark of this issue), for most babies, the valve is loose for a while before the muscles firm up, causing them to spit up. This is normal (as long as the spit-up looks like digested milk, not bright yellow/green or bloody), and although it creates a huge laundry problem, it's not a problem for the baby.

Sometimes, though, if your milk is coming out super fast (called overactive letdown) or if your baby is spitting up all day, every day, it may be uncomfortable for your baby to eat. A lactation specialist can help you assess this and give you tips for positioning and for decreasing the flow to your baby, if necessary.

GETTING THE HELP YOU NEED

About 35 percent of women choose not to breastfeed at all, but for the other 65 percent, 5 percent stop within one week, 18 percent stop within one month, and only a little over 20 percent are still exclusively breastfeeding at six months. Why is this?

There are huge differences between communities around the world with large and small rates of breastfeeding success. In successful communities, virgin breastfeeders have extreme support from experienced breastfeeders. They also expect that breastfeeding will be difficult, and there is no stigma around that difficulty. Sometimes you don't realize the questions or issues you have until an expert helps you out. If you live in a home with all of your breastfeeding friends and experienced breastfeeder family members, you won't need all this outside help, but the reality is that you probably don't live in such a situation.

The solution for many moms in modern America? Hands-on support from a lactation specialist. That way, as long as you recognize the main reasons things don't go well with feeding, you can make adjustments right away, not several days later. Things change really quickly with babies. What is true for their health needs at day 3 can be very different at day 5. So if something is not working well at day 3, you want to catch it really quickly so that it isn't a more major issue two days later.

The best way to get the right lactation help is to know your lactation resources and have them set up before you ever have the baby. Also realize that hospital-based lactation specialists may have a different perspective than someone who primarily cares for babies once they are out of the hospital. Our lactation specialists in clinic see a range of babies from birth to twelve, even twenty-four months, so they feel really comfy moving moms through all the stages of lactation.

Following are the best options for getting lactation help.

In-Home Lactation

If you can swing it, a board-certified lactation specialist that comes to your home multiple times is best. They can assess your individual needs in your home environment. They also should be able to help you as you run into snags to get through them, because they are working directly with you and seeing your home setup.

When you search online to find someone, or ask your friends or future pediatrician, make sure you look for a lactation specialist who has a current International Board-Certified Lactation Consultant status. That way, you'll find someone credible and reliable and who is as up to date as possible on current breastfeeding recommendations.

Clinic-Based Lactation

Call your potential pediatric office to see if they have someone there who can help you. If they have someone that comes into each first visit, great. If not, ask for that once you arrive for your first baby appointment.

Hospital-Based Lactation

These experts are invaluable. Ask for a consult as soon as possible.

Doulas

These can work well if they are board certified in lactation as well as being certified to help with your postpartum care. You're not just looking for opinions here; rather, you want someone who is confident and knows what she is talking about from a trained perspective.

Family Help

This really depends on you. For me, it was really difficult to have a family member hovering around me while I worked on learning how to breastfeed my daughter. It had been thirty-five years since my mother or my mother-in-law breastfed when I had my first baby. They were great support people for things like laundry and meal prep, but their breastfeeding skills were a little rusty.

Online and Book Help

There are a number of great resources online for lactation, but unless they are working with you directly for a consultation, the advice they give in written form will be really generalized and may not accommodate the needs you have. Plus, they won't be with you in-person, obviously, so it may be hard to assess latch or some of the other more nuanced areas of feeding. Online sites, like books, can be a little black and white. Still, it's great to have a starting point. Here are three I find useful:

1. Nancy Mohrbacher (www.nancymohrbacher.com): Her site is not super sleek, but the information is legitimate and super by the book. Again, great for starting out.

2. Lactation Link (www.lactationlink.com): The most intuitive and modern mom-friendly site I've found. She has a free email course and a paid course plus offers online consults. She really knows her stuff. Of note, she does have a partnership with DockATot, which I do not recommend due to suffocation safety concerns.

3. *The Nursing Mother's Companion* by Kathleen Huggins: This is an oldie but goodie. When someone has been doing lactation for twenty-five years, she tends to develop an expertise. Straightforward, good graphics, to the point, a little old-school in some areas so take it with a grain of salt, but totally helpful as a starting place.

Finding lactation help is one of the most important parts of breastfeeding success. You (probably) don't live in a small space with your sisters, your aunts, your mother, and your grandmother who all have breastfeeding prowess. Thank goodness there are caring, professional lactation experts waiting to guide you through the ups and downs of nursing your baby.

WHEN BREASTFEEDING JUST DOESN'T WORK

In this chapter, we talked about what can go wrong with breastfeeding. Breastfeeding failure rates are really high. I'm always trying to help moms reach their breastfeeding goals, but the reality is that it doesn't always go as planned or hoped. If breastfeeding just doesn't work for you, please remember this: being a breastfeeder or a nonbreastfeeder does *not* define you as a mom. It's one small part of your motherhood journey. Being a mom is about *so* much more than breastfeeding.

10

AT HOME IN THE FIRST FEW WEEKS

By the end of next year, you're going to be a seasoned parent. You'll be a pro at a lot of things. Not in that "oh, yeah, babies are hard" kind of way. More like, "I understand that this stage takes exactly two days to pass. I believe it will pass because there was a time three days ago that the very same thing happened and it passed." Things will be etched into your memory:

Initial sleepy stage: 24 hours
Body screaming out in pain as baby learns to latch: 1 week
Breasts engorged and throbbing: 72–90 hours
Fussy period: 2 weeks to 3 months old

You know, that type of thing.

Now, have people written these estimates of time all over the internet? Of course. But if your baby arrives and you feel like none of that made a difference, there's a reason why: it's because it's hard to believe those stages really are just a stage until you've lived through them.

It's like running a long race. If you've run one before, even if it was years ago, it still feels somewhat attainable in the heat of it. On the other hand, if you're a race "virgin," it's kind of hard to believe you will actually come out on the other side without collapsing. If you haven't had a baby before, visualizing what's ahead and asking others about their experiences, plus reading credible information from reliable sources, can make those early days easier.

Still, it is really useful to have at least some basic information about what is normal in the first few weeks so that, when you are caught off guard, you can refer back to it.

KEEPING BABY SAFE

The number one thing moms and dads learn when they become new parents? Not much is under your control. You can, though, take a few steps to set yourself up for as much success as possible.

Get Vaccinated

Making sure that you and the people who come in close contact with your baby have all of their vaccinations is super important. I recommend all of the vaccines on the Centers for Disease Control and Prevention vaccine schedule, but specifically, the whooping cough (pertussis) and flu vaccines (depending on the season) are important for people around you to have.

Stay Away from Sick People

Now is not the time to take your baby to the company picnic or Christmas party. Of course, let your family members hold your new one, but first make sure they are not sick. A crowded Target store trip is not on my list of recommended activities. Instead, take your baby on a short walk in the stroller with an appropriate weather canopy and an extra layer of warmth, if needed.

Hand Washing

Make sure that everyone who touches or holds your baby first thoroughly washes his hands, each time, with warm, soapy water.

Stay Out of the Airport

The first month of a baby's life is not the time to surround yourself with recycled air in an airplane or with a whole host of people you do not know (and their germs) in the airport. How often have you gotten sick after traveling? I don't recommend air travel until babies have had their first set of vaccines (which can happen at six weeks at the earliest).

Falling

Babies can be slippery little suckers. Make sure you have a hand on your baby at all times if they are on an elevated surface. We have, unfortunately, had parents call us multiple times after their babies fell out of beds or off of changing tables. It really freaks me out when I see a baby by herself on an exam table in the office. You never know when she is going to roll slightly or propel herself in one direction or another.

Suffocation

Keep your baby in a safe place for sleep. A lot of new products come and go in the mommy circles. Don't be fooled. Even if "everyone" is using the newest sleep gadget, it doesn't mean it's safe or approved for sleep. Don't add blankets or stuffed animals to the sleep area. Make sure swaddles don't cover the mouth. Avoid side or stomach sleep positions.

YOUR CHANGING INFANT

As your baby grows, your pediatrician will give what we call *anticipatory guidance*, not just to prevent injury and illness but also to help your baby reach his full potential when it comes to development, growth, and whole health.

At each doctor's appointment, we weigh your baby; do a physical exam; and talk with you about what is going well, what you need help with, and what you can expect until the next visit. We also take a look at vaccine status and make sure your baby got the newborn screen in the hospital, that the hearing screen was passed, and that there were no heart concerns while your baby was there.

One of my favorite things to do is see new babies in the office. Remember, your doctor is there to help you and guide you as you navigate those challenging early days.

The first two weeks are all about—you guessed it—getting the feeding right. Babies tend to do a lot of cluster feeding during these weeks, where they just finished feeding and then seem to want to feed again twenty minutes later. They also sleep sporadically and are just getting used to their environment outside the womb. Here are the top four things parents consistently tell me are painful about those first two weeks and what you can do to address them.

Diaper Rashes

Why?

Diaper rashes are really common because your baby's skin is about thirty times more sensitive than an adult's. The diaper area is dark and warm and wet—the perfect place for yeast and bacteria to breed. Your baby is (hopefully) pooping and peeing all day long. Plus, the materials in most baby wipes can be super irritating, even if they are labeled as natural.

What can you do about it?

Change diapers right away. If your baby is sleeping and has a pee diaper, don't feel like you need to wake her up to change it. But otherwise, you want to get that acid and those irritants off your baby's skin as fast as possible.

Use diaper creams with a barrier component as soon as possible at the first sign of a rash, and use them with *each* diaper change until the rash goes away. My go-to is usually good ol' Desitin. Apply that stuff like cupcake frosting—you want a thick barrier so that the next time your baby urinates, the skin doesn't get even more irritated, preventing healing.

Choose good wipes. Pampers Sensitive or Water Wipes tend to work well. A lot of parents get really excited about fancy wipes. Unfortunately, even wipes that are labeled as organic or natural can have products in them that really irritate a baby's bottom. This is an area where basic is better.

Ask your doctor if the rash doesn't start to go away after a few days or it looks different than just redness or irritation. They can help you figure out if you need medicine for yeast or bacteria.

Spit-Up

Why?

It's normal for all babies to spit up, and most of the time, it is just a laundry issue. Every once in a while, though, it can cause discomfort for babies and can make successful breastfeeding difficult.

What can you do about it?

Hold your baby upright after feeds. This allows the food to go down versus up. Think about yourself when you eat a huge meal or down a huge beer. You feel nasty, right? You feel like burping. You might even feel a little bit of spit-up coming up. If you were to lie down, you would feel even worse. The same goes for a baby. Experts recommend an upright position after feeds as much as possible.

Burp your baby often during feeds. This allows the air bubbles to come up and the food to go down.

If you are using a bottle, use a slower-flow nipple. This creates less of a firehose scenario for your baby when she is trying to feed.

If you are breastfeeding, ask your doctor or lactation specialist about laid-back positioning and about c-clamping if it seems like you may have overactive letdown. Signs are that it seems like your baby is having a hard time handling the amount of milk that comes into his mouth or, when your breasts let down, it seems that milk sprays everywhere or you have so much milk on your initial letdown that you have to catch a bunch of it in a towel/it gets all over you and your baby.

Laid-back nursing positioning is just that—you recline back onto a pillow or a couch so that you're at more of a 45-degree angle with your baby, as opposed to leaning over your baby's mouth, so that the milk flows more like a stream versus like a waterfall (which is less forceful).

C-clamping is when you make a c-shape with your forefinger and your thumb, encircling your breast just behind the areola. You latch your baby, watch the baby swallow your first letdown's milk, and then, instead of clamping down and pushing forward, you clamp down and push back on the breast tissue to stop the flow. Wait until baby takes a pause from eating, then loosen your clamp. Repeat this for the rest of the feed until baby is done eating. Again, your pediatrician or lactation consultant will be the best person to let you know if this is appropriate for you.

Superhuman Levels of Fatigue

When you are a new parent, sleep deprivation is your biggest enemy. If you can get the sleep you need, everything is much better.

Why?

You're all hyped up on hormones and anxiety. In the very beginning, the adrenaline coursing through your body really messes with your sleep. Sometimes you notice every little sound your baby makes, making it really difficult to get the shut-eye you need. By the time all that dies down, you're left exhausted and behind the eight ball.

Plus, you tend to have a lot of family around. At my core, I am an introvert, and that personality trait did not change the second I had a baby. If you are an introvert, too, the same will be true for you. In fact, your natural tendency will probably get stronger.

When you have a new little one, people want to make you dinner and help as much as possible. They want to see the new baby. Family, especially, wants to spend precious time with you right away. They also want to socialize with you. They are excited about your bundle of joy and want to talk all about it.

Add in the fact that your baby snoozes all day and is awake all night, and *boom!*—the perfect recipe for disaster.

Sometimes the daytime sleeping tricks you into feeling like you should or could get a bunch done during the day. Your energy is up, and you feel like you might as well get out of the house or at least put in a load of laundry. But then nighttime comes and everything goes haywire. Unless the help you have in your house is there to be on night duty, it's just you (and your partner, I hope) up all night trying to figure things out and not disturb your houseguests.

What can you do about it?

Have times in the first few weeks *every day* when you are completely off-duty except to feed. Put in ear plugs, go to a separate area of the house, and have your partner come get you up when baby needs to eat, but otherwise, be free in your own home, even if it is for five minutes.

Before the nighttime craziness gets going, rest. It sounds lame, but going to bed at about 7 pm, after you do your last evening feeding, allows you get in a solid one or two (maybe three) hours before the night shift starts. Have the baby resting in the main room (in a safe American Academy of Pediatrics-approved sleeping space) for that time so you can't hear all those little sweet noises and you get some solid shut-eye. Then, when you get worked up again a few hours later, you know you at least have those few hours under your belt.

I did not do that with my first daughter, but with my second, I made it a point to, and it was a *game-changer*. It really took the fear out of the nighttime sleep situation.

Baby Blobbiness

Definition: The feeling that your baby is a blob but you want to do something to stimulate him or her.

What can you do about it?

Read, read, read. It doesn't have to be baby books in the first few weeks to month. Read your own novels out loud. Reading and talking to our children enhances communication, reducing frustrations as they learn to ask for what they want and need but also fostering social connections and building parent-baby bonds. Research shows that the more words parents use when speaking to an eight-month-old infant (it can be a difference of thirty million words from one family to another!), the greater the size of the child's vocabulary at age three.

I love having background music on in the house. Both of my babies went to multiple concerts when they were in my belly, and they'd been out dancing and swaying before they came into the world. The best thing for them, though, is when they actually hear the people they love singing to them, looking in their eyes, or dancing around with them.

Find information about age-appropriate activities you can do with your child, but remember that the basics are still the most important. Here are two apps I've found that give helpful info to new parents about baby development.

The Wonder Weeks

The Wonder Weeks is a book (and an app) that gives you activities you can do with your baby based on her due date and the date she was actually born. I like this app because it goes through what a baby's mind is capable of comprehending at that time, not just "show them black-and-white picture books" with no explanation. The book and app also talk about developmental leaps, and they try to predict when your baby will be fussy based on your baby's age. The most important aspect of *The Wonder Weeks* is the development information.

Baby Sparks

Baby Sparks also gives you developmental play suggestions (up to two years old), but it is a lot more pricey. It is the Cadillac of developmental play apps. If you're super into knowing everything possible about development, it's a great option. One nice feature is that you have lifetime access if you download the app (presumably to use with your second or third child), but the reality is that once you get to baby number two or three, you'll have the basics down, and you may not need this level of developmental information to feel confident. In fact, your worries may be placed more on how to support your baby's older siblings or how to keep your new baby safe from older kids at that time.

NIGHTTIME SLEEP

They were straight-up petrified. A mom- and dad-to-be, sitting there on the couch in my pediatrics office. Wide-eyed and hopeful, hopped up on information about "this year's best stroller." Filled to the brim with platitudes their friends and family all offered about what to expect when the timer went "ding" on their little bun in the oven. "It'll be hard, but you'll love it. Enjoy your sleep now, 'cause it will never be the same again."

They had heard it all for months, and now they were looking for *real* answers as to what would happen to their lives in those first few weeks, for the steps they actually could take to prepare themselves for the new little baby that was about to enter their world and turn it completely upside down.

I see it all the time in prenatal meet-and-greet appointments in my clinic—the fear, the trepidation, to bring up the main question that is on (pretty much) everyone's mind: how do I get this baby to sleep, and how do I get her to sleep "like a baby"? Good news is, I've got the answer.

Before we get to the strategy part, these four bits of knowledge are key.

Babies Don't Get It

Babies don't realize we're living in the modern world. They have no idea that you have a limited maternity leave. It doesn't matter to them that you've already lived thirty-five years and have a social life. They certainly don't care if you have a certain level of sleep you're used to. Their needs and desires are the same as the needs babies had thousands of years ago.

When they are first born (and for the first three months afterward), they want only to keep things going as they were in that blissful, dark, loud, warm, cozy womb from which they just came. Dr. Harvey Karp wrote all about their primitive needs in his groundbreaking book *The Happiest Baby on the Block*. It's over twenty years old at this point, but its age doesn't matter, because *babies haven't changed one bit* since then. The principles are just as true now as they were back in the day.

Babies Are Mixed Up

They also have their days and nights completely switched up. Before birth, your baby is swayed by the motion of your body throughout the day, lulled to sleep by the small and large movements you make. At night, it's party time. If you are pregnant and reading this right now, you know *exactly* what I mean. It's reassuring on some level to feel a baby kicking around all night long, but it's also hard to get any shut-eye some nights. All throughout the night, your body is not in motion, and so your baby thinks it's time to get active. After baby comes out, it takes awhile for your newborn to get the drift that night is actually night and day is actually day.

You Do Get It

You do realize you live in the modern world. I know, I know, you already know that. That's why you're so scared about this in the first place, right? But a new parent's perspective gets thwarted easily. Somewhere along the line, people tend to forget this basic premise: this is not like all the modern things you normally do. They start trying to fix things instead. They try to make their baby get on a sleep schedule starting week 1 (I do think that bedtime routines and sleep schedules can be a great thing, they're just not the solution really early on for most babies). They buy every product known to man. They fight and fight and fight baby sleep.

I've been there. I've searched for hours and hours for the perfect sleep solution. I've gotten frustrated with my baby, with my partner, and with the whole stinkin' situation. I've lost sight of the fact that sometimes you can't fix it. You just have to let it ride out.

Let me give you a nonbaby example: think of the last really challenging exercise class or workout you did. The one where you had to psych yourself up even to make it down to the studio or to strap on those running shoes, because you just *knew* that there would be a moment when you'd think, "This is so hard." Think of the moment you had to tell yourself, "Just keep breathing, use your resources (distracting yourself with music, focusing on your form, thinking about your goal)." Think about how, at some point, your options were to give up or to keep pushing through.

There wasn't anything you could do to make it substantially better; you just had to keep going. That's kind of how, on some level, you have to approach new baby sleep. In the beginning, there are only so many things you can control (we'll get to these in a second). Instead, you have to focus more on your own resources so that *you* can get through the tough time with resilience.

Babies Don't Always Follow the Book

Your baby may not do what the baby sleep books tells him to do. If someone tells you that she can get *every* baby to sleep well *every night* using her methods, you've gotta be a little wary. I mean, come on, you are smart enough never to buy that when it comes to anything else in your life (think get-rich-quick schemes, perfect beauty tricks), so why would it be true for baby sleep, when families and children are all so individual? No, babies are like Frank Sinatra—they do it *their way*.

A child's temperament is a huge influencer of how well he sleeps from the very, very beginning. Environment and parents sure help, but in the end, temperament always plays a huge role. Some babies are just better sleepers than others. My first baby was all kinds of colicky. She just did *not* sleep at night. I worked and worked and worked at it, and eventually she got it down, but it was definitely a full-time job for a while. My second daughter, on the other hand, followed the baby sleep handbook. She fell asleep easily, woke happy, and then did it all again a few hours later.

I'm not telling you this to scare you. I'm telling you because, if you have a baby who doesn't like to sleep or has a hard time getting into the rhythm, you shouldn't beat yourself up about it. It is not your fault. It's just the way your sweet boy or girl is wired. One day, he or she will probably be CEO of a Fortune 500 company. But for those first five to six months of life, it might be a little rough in the sleep department. Repeat after me: "I *will* get through this."

Feeling defeated? Don't. There is a way to get through the throes of newborn sleeplessness with grace and resilience.

Set Yourself Up for Success

Create an environment that is conducive to good sleep at night. Make the room dark; get the white noise going. Read *Happiest Baby on the Block* from cover to cover. Then read it again. Watch YouTube videos of how to soothe your baby.

Don't expect that it, like any other book, will work perfectly, but expect it to give you a place to start when baby gets really worked up and won't rest. You want to avoid feeling stuck, like you have no tricks up your sleeve. Get the basics down ahead of time and add to your toolbox as you go, making lists of calming tricks if you need to and putting them on your fridge or phone so you can refer to them as you get familiar with what works for your baby.

The American Academy of Pediatrics recommends that babies be put to bed by themselves on their backs on a flat surface with a tightly fitted sheet and no extra bedding or pillows to prevent sudden infant death syndrome (SIDS). I wholeheartedly agree with this recommendation.

If you use something other than a swaddle blanket to wrap your baby, you'll likely look on a site like Amazon for advice on what to purchase. Like most other gear for babies, if an item gets ten thousand 5-star Amazon reviews, it's a great place to start, but it still might not be the best for *your* baby. You might have to try things out to see what will work for you and your family. Remember to check out safety information on sites like Consumer Reports—just because something is available online does not mean that it is a safe product for a baby.

Remember to transition your baby to a product like a sleep sack with the arms free by two months. Your baby learns how to roll around this time and may accidentally flip onto his belly and not be able to get back over if he is swaddled.

Address Your Own Sleep Needs

This is the most important tip I can give you about newborn sleep. When I finished residency, I thought I would be all set to deal with sleep deprivation. I was used to staying up all night long, sometimes for up to thirty hours at a time for one shift. But the thing I forgot when I got into the whole new-baby thing was the fact that I was also accustomed, at some point, to having uninterrupted rest for hours at a time. Plus some weekends off. That is very different from the sinking feeling that you may never sleep again when your infant is brand new. While you can't completely control how your baby sleeps, you can make sure you optimize your own sleep. Here's how.

You need to feed your baby really frequently in the early days and weeks, but you don't need to be the only one who soothes her in between feeding sessions. That means your partner (or someone else—a family member, a postpartum doula) needs to step in and become "soother-in-chief" for a while. Otherwise, you will be at higher risk for postpartum depression and anxiety, resent the people around you, and be less able to enjoy your baby during the day. If (again, back to our ancestors) you lived with all twenty of your favorite relatives in one common dwelling, this would be easy. In our culture of isolation, it can be tricky for some new moms to find help, but it is so very worth it.

Even if you have someone designated as a soother every other night for one week, it will do wonders for your mental and physical health. The whole point is having a time in the future you can look forward to when you know you will get sleep (even if that time is two days away).

Put to Sleep Awake

While your baby is still in the snoozy phase, try sometimes to put your baby to sleep while he is still slightly awake so that he gets used to falling asleep on his own.

Plan Ahead for Potential Co-sleeping

There are some times when you will likely fall asleep with your baby. You need to make sure that, if you do co-sleep, you've taken appropriate action to make sure it's done safely. No one who is high or drunk should sleep in the bed. Remove all blankets and pillows. Make sure the mattress is firm. Set up a system so that baby does not fall off the bed.

Wait It Out

Be patient with your baby and with yourself. For some babies, sleep is great right away, but for others, you've got to wade through the murky water until you get to the fresh stream a little farther ahead. Use your resources and mindfulness, just like you would for any other challenging obstacle in your life. Of course, if your baby seems excessively fussy or you are concerned about illness, seek help from your child's pediatrician. Get help from a lactation consultant if things seem to be haywire in the feeding department.

So, is it possible for a newborn to sleep like a baby? Well, technically, yes. They will sleep like the immature, womb-seeking, still-developing humans that they are. That's the truth. Remember how primitive your baby's needs are. Get your mind right. Get educated about how to soothe a baby and set up a sleep environment that optimizes rest for both of you. Above all, because babies aren't modernizing anytime soon, make sure you get *your* sleep by forming a solid team around you from the get-go. That way, even if your baby isn't quite up to speed on how to calm and sleep when he first arrives, you can teach him with patience and perspective until he finds his way.

DAYTIME SLEEP AND CARRYING

During the day, products like the Rock 'n' Play Sleeper and baby swings can be super helpful if you are observing your baby in them and the baby is awake. Just remember that your goal is to get your baby to have less rocking and swaying during the day once you get your rhythm with feeding, so some times without those products are great. Also, they are not designed for sleep.

Wearing your baby has also been proven to reduce colic and, obviously, to help you bond with your baby.

There are a lot of options out there for carriers—I'm going to be honest and say that the long-piece-of-fabric varieties just never worked for me. I watched many tutorial videos on how to put them on, but my babies always hated them. The good news? This is an area where the sky's the limit, and the baby blogs are full of reviews.

SOOTHING

He was holding her like she might bite him, his arms outstretched and awkward, shoulders tense. The baby was crying, her arms also outstretched and flailing, as he tried to half bounce, half shush her. It was almost painful to watch.

"She doesn't like me. She only wants her mom," he told me at our first well-baby checkup in the office. "I've never been around babies. I don't have any clue what to do with them."

His face looked lost, surprised, defeated. He felt like he could not contribute and wondered if he would ever bond with the little alien being who had just arrived via his wife's body. (I know this sounds crazy, but the things that go through your mind as a new parent often are.)

My husband said he felt the same way when he held my daughter for the first time. Many new parents tell me they feel this way, and unfortunately, it can be a self-perpetuating cycle of defeat when you feel like each time it's your turn to soothe your baby, your baby somehow gets crankier and crankier. You know how they say bees can smell fear? It's clear that newborn babies can, too. Well, maybe not smell it, but at least they can sense it. If you're not relaxed as you try to relax them, they know it.

We spent fifteen minutes that day walking through the basics of soothing a baby. In the end, he was by no means the baby whisperer, but he did have the information and tools he needed to keep trying to bond with his little one.

Soothing your baby falls into two categories: getting ahold of yourself and then attending to your baby. You've heard the phrase on an airplane "Put the mask on yourself first"? That applies here as well. Earlier, we talked about getting your mindset right when it comes to having a baby. Here we'll talk about soothing your little one.

Dr. Harvey Karp wrote all about what he refers to as the fourth trimester in *Happiest Baby on the Block*. The basic premise is that babies are not quite ready to be in this world when they come out and that, given their neurodevelopmental immaturity, they are more easily stimulated and irritated by the stress of the outside world.

Our goal as parents should be to mimic the intrauterine environment from which they just came, which is dark, very loud (think blood rushing around and a loud heartbeat), almost constantly in motion (except when you are sleeping—that's why babies tend to be more active in the evenings), and quite compact and secure.

You can re-create that feeling of security by using what he calls the 5 *S*s:

1. Swaddling
2. Sucking
3. *Shhhhh* . . .
4. Swinging
5. Side or Stomach Positioning (not safe sleep positions, great for soothing when awake)

She was already crying when I opened the door to the exam room. She sat defeated, her newborn baby snuggled closely in her arms, huge tears slipping down her cheeks. Try as she might, she could not get the latch right when she tried to nurse. She told me she must be one of those "breastfeeding failures." She had spent the last four days in pain as her baby clamped down on her again and again. Now, exhausted and defeated, she wasn't sure how to move forward.

I watched as she told me her story, her shoulders heaving as she took gulping breaths between sobs. I knew what she really meant: "I feel like I have already failed at this whole mother thing and I am less than a week into it. I am not the parent I'd hoped I would be."

Disappointment

Breastfeeding is a parenting area ripe for disappointment. We put a ton of pressure on mothers-to-be, then don't educate them well before their babies are born on the potential pitfalls of this not-so-intuitive task. After birth, support from other experienced breastfeeders is usually minimal at home. Add in that we often put the onus on moms to do most of the day and night care within a family, and *bam!*—Stress City, here we come.

Of course, I get and support the Breast Is Best movement when possible. The benefits of breast milk and breastfeeding are super clear, and I want to help nursing parents reach their breastfeeding goals. But those who cannot or do not breastfeed often feel (or are made to feel) like they are somehow parenting failures because of their struggles or decisions in this *one area*.

Breastfeeding is not the only opportunity to feel, potentially, like a parenting failure. What about when we raise our voice at our toddler when we're stressed or realize we've been ignoring our baby while we peruse our social media feed? How about the time my doctor friend missed her own kid's case of pneumonia? Yeah, those feel like real "Mother of the Year" moments, too.

The Real Fears

What about the bigger, longer-term fears we all have? That the core issues we deal with ourselves are going to royally ruin our kids in some way? Your mild anxiety (or your a-little-too-laid-back personality), your own parents' failures, your lack of expertise in all things child related—all of these insecurities can get in the way of doing your best day by day.

One mom in my office put it so well: "I handle multi-million-dollar sales transactions on a daily basis. I sit in a conference room with other business leaders and can influence their decision-making at the drop of a hat. But getting my toddler to put on her shirt? Somehow, I fail every day at doing that without getting flustered and losing my cool. It's so demoralizing. I'm scared of what I'll mess up when she gets older and it really counts."

Social media feeds our worries on this as well. You've seen the articles: "10 Things That Will Mess Up Your Relationship with Your Teenager," "The 5 Tips You Need to Raise Brave Girls." They are well intentioned, and they often have really useful information, but read enough of them and, in the end, they can leave you feeling stuck, not motivated, if consumed without the right perspective.

Our friends, our parents, our significant others—pressure and guilt can come from all sides, piling on a sense that it's all or nothing. That good enough is never enough. That only the best will do.

The real secret to successful parenting is understanding and dealing with our own personal struggles and pain points, not pretending they don't exist or acting like, if we just smile a little brighter, others won't notice our humanity. Going to therapy, or to lactation, or to the pediatrician for help. Understanding we are not as in control as we think we are most of the time. That sometimes we do our best and take all the classes and read all the books and *it still doesn't work*. Taking a look at our own "weaknesses" and fears—these are the things that really make a difference.

I looked that sobbing mom in the eye, took her hands, and told her what countless moms (including me) have needed to hear at some time or another: "You are an amazing mother. What or how you feed your child does not define that. In fact, you can use the fact that you overcame this challenge (either breastfeeding in the end *or not*) to show your baby how to be resilient in his own life. All moms have moments when they realize it is impossible to be flawless and that it is better, in the end, not to be. You are more than okay. You are just what your baby needs."

Of course, that's when I started tearing up right alongside her.

I knew some reassurance would help, but the look of relief that washed across that new mom's face? It was stunning to see her whole body relax and her demeanor change.

Baby and mom ended up just fine. They found their way. We got mom the help she needed, but more importantly, we addressed one of the most foundational worries of motherhood directly.

IN CONCLUSION

The Day Your Baby Arrives

You are going to be an amazing mom. Not a perfect mom, but an amazing one. Remember that on your best days and on your worst days. Remind yourself that your baby is specifically meant to be yours. Don't beat yourself up if, just a few days or weeks into this thing called motherhood, you do not feel like you are the parent you'd hoped you would be. None of us is.

Try your best. Deal with your own issues head-on; get the help you need to support yourself and give you the parenting tools that will allow you to rise above your most challenging days. Your children will thank you for it when they're navigating their own parenting paths years down the road.

SECTION III

SELF-CARE GUIDES AND
NEWBORN CARE RESOURCES

DEVELOPING YOUR PRIORITIES GUIDE

Following are activities we all spend time on, arranged randomly.

Work
Homemaking
Kids
Hobbies
Spouse
Appearance
Friendships
Exercise/Stress Reduction
Travel/Experiences

Rank these activities in order based on what you, in an ideal world, would spend the most time on/doing. Rank them as a private, honest list, not based on how you think other people would want you to rank them or how you think you should rank them.

IDEAL LIST:

_____
_____
_____
_____
_____
_____
_____
_____
_____

Now, rank the activities based on what you actually spend time on throughout the week or month.

REALITY LIST:

_____

_____

_____

_____

_____

_____

_____

_____

_____

Compare your first list (your Ideal List) with the second list (your Reality List). How do they match up? Use the top three items on your Ideal List to help you determine a self-care ritual.

PARTNER CARE PLANNING GUIDE

List several activities you and your partner each like to do individually.

YOU:

_____

_____

PARTNER:

_____

_____

List four experience activities you and your partner could do locally together (think beyond dinner and a movie, for example, concerts, hikes).

_____

_____

_____

_____

List four bigger experience activities you and your partner could do together (trips, events).

_____

_____

_____

_____

POTENTIAL CHILDCARE OPTIONS?

POTENTIAL BARRIERS

SELF-CARE GOAL SETTING

Self-care doesn't happen by accident, it happens by design. Follow these steps to make your self-care goals.

REFLECT AND EVALUATE

Think about what makes you happy in your life right now when it comes to self-care. Write out the top five things (your happy list) and then the top five things you wish were different (your wish list).

Sample Lists

Happy List

> I enjoy special outings with my kids.
> I see my friends once every two weeks at social, kid-related activities.
> I have date nights with my husband occasionally.
> I feel great when I take time to practice yoga or go for a walk outside.
> My husband and I travel occasionally together.

Wish List

> I want to be more physically fit.
> I want to have more time where I'm quiet without distractions.
> I want to travel more often.
> I want to pursue my passions, things I used to spend time on before I had kids (writing, learning guitar, and learning about cooking).
> I want to have more energy throughout the day.

Happy List:

1._____

2._____

3._____

4._____

5._____

Wish List:

1._____

2._____

3._____

4._____

5._____

SET SMART GOALS

Then, set three SMART self-care goals based on your wish list: SMART Goals are Specific, Measurable, Attainable, Realistic and Time-Sensitive.

Specific

It's not worth it to have something like, "I want to feel better about myself" as a goal. Feeling better is a good starting place, but it's just too ambiguous. There is no way to tell if you've actually achieved your goal once you get there.

Measurable

Measurable goals have an outcome you can assess after a certain amount of time to determine your level of progress. That way, you know when you've met your goal and are ready to set a new goal.

Attainable

If you set a goal that is too far out of reach, the chances of you reaching that goal are pretty slim. For example, an unattainable goal for me would be, "I will be a marathon runner next month." Instead, "I will complete a 10k run in three months" is not so daunting.

Realistic

Realistic goals are goals that are not based in fantasy. Instead, they are possible to achieve, even if it takes several steps to accomplish them. For example, I could set a self-care goal of going to Italy five times a year but I know that's not going to happen (I can't take that much time off work, I don't have the money for it, and I wouldn't have the childcare resources for it). A more realistic goal? Going out of town with my husband (to a local venue or somewhere a short plane trip away) three times per year. We may have to save money to do it or I might have to work a little extra to make it happen, but it's something that I know is not completely far-fetched if I plan ahead and make it a priority.

Time

Even with self-care goals, time is an important element. If my desire is to be more physically fit and my goal is to work out more to achieve that goal, I need to set a timeline, so I can get organized and motivate myself to actually make the change. For example, "My goal is to write a children's book by one year from now. I'll do step x by 1 month from now, step y by two months from now and step z by three months from now to work toward that goal."

Breaking our goals into smaller steps makes it even more likely we'll achieve them.

Step 1

_____

_____

Step 2

_____

_____

Common Developmental Milestones in the First Year	
2 Weeks	-Responding to Sounds -Gazing at Face or Bold Prints -Improved Head Control and Neck Rotation
2 Months	-Smiling -Cooing -Observing and Listening -Improved Head Control and Neck Rotation -Interest in Mobiles and Activity Mats
4 Months	-Laughing -Babbling -Batting at Objects -Learning to Roll -Increased Interest in Moving Objects to Mouth
6 Months	-Practicing Sitting Up -Rolling Both Directions -Squealing, Screaming, Happy Vocalizations -Turning in the Direction of Noise -Improved Ability to Grasp -Transferring Objects Between Hands
9 Months	-Increased Movement (Crawling, Creeping or Pulling to Stand) -Starting to Say "Mama" or "Dada" -Developing Pincer Grasp with Thumb and Forefinger
12 Months	-Improved Mobility (Cruising, Walking or Crawling) -Understanding Words -Improved Pincer Grasp -Starting to Use Words Consistently

*All children develop differently. Ask your pediatrician for help with assessing your child's development.

Expected Vaccine Schedule in the First Year	
Birth	Hepatitis B #1
2 Months	Diphtheria, Pertussis, Tetanus (DTap) #1 Haemophilus Influenzae Type B (Hib) #1 Pneumococcal Conjugate (PCV13 or Prevnar 13) #1 Rotavirus #1 Hepatitis B #2
4 Months	Diphtheria, Pertussis, Tetanus (DTap) #2 Haemophilus Influenzae Type B (Hib) #2 Pneumococcal Conjugate (PCV13 or Prevnar 13) #2 Rotavirus #2
6 Months	Diphtheria, Pertussis, Tetanus (DTap) #3 Haemophilus Influenzae Type B (Hib) #3 Pneumococcal Conjugate (PCV13 or Prevnar 13) #3 Rotavirus #3
9 Months	Hepatitis B #3
12 Months	Varicella (Chickenpox) #1 Hepatitis A #1

*This schedule may vary slightly according to clinic. Ask your pediatrician for clinic-specific vaccine administration policies.

ABOUT
MODERN MOMMY DOC

Follow Dr. Casares at www.modernmommydoc.com. All of us want to be great parents. We're here to help you do it. It's possible to raise resilient, healthy children that contribute to their communities and have a sense of purpose. *How?* Successful parents:

- Manage their expectations
- Understand child development
- Respond versus react
- Promote strengths and accept weaknesses
- Address their own issues
- Have the right priorities
- Focus on resilience
- Make time for themselves

Good parenting is about information, resources, and perspective. My goal is to give you all three.

NOTES

NOTES

NOTES

Made in the USA
Middletown, DE
21 November 2018